The Gospels
for Your Whole Life

Mark and John in Prayer and Study

William G. Thompson

WINSTON PRESS

For Mary Sharon Riley:
religious of the Cenacle, colleague in ministry,
faithful friend

Cover design: Art Direction Inc.

Library of Congress Catalog Card Number: 82-51241

ISBN: 0-86683-645-4

Printed in the United States of America

5 4 3 2 1

Winston Press, Inc.
430 Oak Grove
Minneapolis, Minnesota 55403

Contents

Acknowledgments

Reflecting on the people I wish to acknowledge for their contribution to this book, I was drawn to ask how I came to write it. The book began with my doctoral studies in the New Testament at the Biblical Institute in Rome during the Second Vatican Council. In those studies I learned the historical and literary methods as they applied to the gospels, and I gained a deep respect for the technical research and scholarly publication that characterized my work at that time. I am grateful to all of my teachers, most especially William L. Moran, professor of Old Testament.

From 1967 to 1981 I taught New Testament at the Jesuit School of Theology in Chicago and in the summer sessions at the Loyola University Institute of Pastoral Studies. Through basic courses in the gospels I began to relate what I had learned in my doctoral studies to adult spirituality and pastoral ministry. In other courses I brought the New Testament writings into dialogue with psychology and spirituality, myth and symbol, religious experience, images of God, and styles of prayer. I wish to thank the students who, perhaps without knowing it, greatly encouraged and challenged me to pursue the work that has come to written expression in this book.

My New Testament colleagues will recognize how much they have contributed to this book. I am especially indebted to Paul J. Achtemeier, Raymond E. Brown, Sean Freyne, Robert Kysar, and Norman Peterson.

A strong contributor to my development has been David C. Reeves. On two occasions we collaborated in teaching a course entitled "Myth and Symbol in the Bible." Recognizing the strengths and limitations of the historical-critical approach to the Bible, we attempted to blend historical-critical data with symbolic metaphorical and mythic activity. David's exceptional gifts in dealing with complex concepts and theory balanced my strengths in spirituality and pastoral ministry. I gladly acknowledge how much he taught me in that collaboration, and how much of what I learned informs this book.

From 1967 to 1981 I also taught courses on scripture and the spirituality of St. Ignatius Loyola. In these courses, I attempted to integrate my knowledge of the New Testament and the spiritual tradition I cherish as a Jesuit. I am indebted to James J. Doyle, S.J., and Kenneth G. Galbraith, S.J., whose knowledge, understanding, and appreciation of Ignatian spirituality enriched the courses we taught together.

In my search for a tool to interpret the New Testament to adult readers and to introduce adult readers to the text, I discovered contemporary psychological theories of adult development. I discovered James W. Fowler's earliest writings on faith development, and I have enjoyed a strong personal and professional relationship with him over the past several years. Jim has shown me how to be a deeply caring man in the academic world, and his understanding of faith development has enriched my understanding of gospel-centered prayer. I am deeply indebted to Jim Fowler, for his theories inform this book, and his colleagueship and friendship have inspired me to integrate adult development with the gospels of Mark and John.

I met Evelyn and James Whitehead at the Institute of Pastoral Studies, and since the early seventies we have shared inspiration and encouragement, support and challenge. Through their writings I have come to value their work on adult Christianity. This book endeavors to bring the Whiteheads' patterns of adult Christian life into dialogue with the gospels of Mark and John.

Since the early seventies I have conducted workshops, prayer-study weekends, and retreats and have given lectures on the New Testament in adult spirituality and pastoral ministry in the United States, Canada, India, Indonesia, Australia, and New Zealand. The material for this book has grown out of and has been tested in these varied adult education settings. I am grateful to the laity and religious, ministers and priests whose enthusiastic response has helped shape the material and bring it to this written form.

Yvette Nelson, editor for Winston Press, has acted as my objective and critical public. Her thorough editing has helped me bring my original manuscript closer to its intended readers. Linda Condon, administrative assistant at Loyola's Institute of

Pastoral Studies, typed and retyped the manuscript with patience, interest, and dedication. To both of them I am most grateful.

Finally, I am happy to dedicate this book to Mary Sharon Riley, r.c. Mary Sharon dreamed the original dream with me and has supported me in making that dream a reality. Her skill in helping adults get to know and pray the gospels has guided the preparation and organization of the book, and she has contributed the concrete cases and general reflections on prayer out of her rich ministry in spiritual direction and directed retreats. Above all, Mary Sharon's personal conviction and enthusiasm have kept me at work when my faith grew dim. She has been a true colleague in ministry as well as a faithful friend.

Introduction

"How can we get started and help others get started with the gospels? How do we deepen our religious appreciation of these writings?" I have heard these questions asked by laity and religious, priests and ministers, in parishes, in workshops, and in scripture classes for adults, and I have written this book in response to these questions. To respond briefly, I would say that getting started with and deepening your religious appreciation of the gospels means *getting to know, praying with,* and *studying the gospels.*

Through *getting to know* the gospels, you can become familiar enough with them to feel at ease with them. By *praying with* the gospels, you can live and grow with them as you live and grow with a friend; you can come to cherish and appreciate them as the word of God. Then, gradually through further *study* you can learn about their historical setting and enter more deeply into their stories. In this book, then, I want to describe a process for getting to know, praying with, and studying Mark and John.

The following experience helped me see what it means to invite you to appreciate Mark and John. One sunny afternoon in the third year of my doctoral studies at the Biblical Institute in Rome, I visited the nearby Museo Nationale. I entered a long, narrow room flooded with light that poured in from a row of windows to my left. On the long wall to my right hung a large rectangular oil by Tintoretto. The intense sunlight created a glare on the canvas that made it impossible for me to see the painting. Frustrated, I began to move on to the next room, when a museum guard shouted from behind me, "Momento! Momento!" He called me back into the room and lowered the shades to dim the bright light. Then he moved me to a spot in front of the Tintoretto painting and said, "Now look." I looked, and I saw what I had been unable to see before. I was drawn so deeply into the painting that I lost all sense of time.

Eventually the guard returned, and in the course of our conversation he told me about Tintoretto—the historical setting in which he painted, the influences upon him, his techniques, the various elements that gave the painting its beauty and power. This information about the painting greatly enriched my initial appreciation. Moreover, by controlling the light and selecting for me the optimum vantage point from which to view the painting, the guard had done me the added favor of sharing with me his own love for and knowledge about the painting.

My work with the New Testament has enabled me to do for others—with their cooperation—what the museum guard did for me that sunny day in Rome. Like him, I can create an environment and suggest a position from which you can discover the richness of Mark and John. I can give you hints about their literary structure and describe their dramatic movement. But you alone can read these gospels and let yourselves become enchanted. I can reflect on what it means to pray with Mark and John and suggest methods for such prayer. But you alone can grow intimate with these gospels and participate in them through prayer. I can provide information about the historical setting in which these gospels were written, and I can describe for you their dominant symbols, metaphors, and themes. But you alone can study Mark and John and let this information enrich your appreciation.

So, I invite you to get to know the gospels of Mark and John, to pray with them, and to study them as though you were meeting them for the first time. Chapters 1 and 5 will introduce you to each gospel and will provide you with a fresh starting point. I invite you to set aside previous images of these two gospels so that you can meet them directly, not as others may have told you about them. In getting to know these gospels, you will find yourself interacting with the texts and asking questions such as: What aspects of Mark and John do I like most? What do I find especially meaningful for me? What characters do I find myself ignoring? What do I react to most strongly in Mark and John? But final answers to these questions will be available only after you have prayed with and studied these gospels further.

Once you have been introduced to the gospels of Mark and John, you may want to use them for prayer. Chapters 2 and 6 describe prayer as a personal encounter in love between God and ourselves and point out that the desire to encounter and respond to God's call to prayer is itself a gift.

Prayer requires that we set aside time to be with God and that we develop the art of listening for God to speak to us. Chapters 2 and 6 present concrete cases of people praying with Mark and John and offer reflections on the methods these people model.

Chapters 3 and 7 describe the background of Mark and John— the worlds behind these gospels, the concrete historical situation in which they originated. What was that situation? How did each gospel come to be? What did this gospel mean to the evangelist and the people for whom he wrote? Does that situation resemble our present situation? In answering these questions we will gain a "feel" for each gospel and gradually enter into dialogue with its human setting.

Chapters 4 and 8 study Mark and John in themselves. My goal will be to help you deepen your relationship with these gospels and enhance the religious appreciation you will gain through prayer. I will explore each evangelist's distinctive stories about Jesus of Nazareth. Through symbols and metaphors, through literary forms and dramatic movement, each gospel discloses a portrait of Jesus teaching and healing, relating to followers and enemies, dying and rising from the dead. In each drama, Jesus discloses values and principles, visions and dreams that together create a way to make meaning in our lives. I invite you to enter each gospel's distinctive story with the expectation that you might gradually find yourself at home there.

The three activities—getting to know, praying with, and studying the gospels—frequently happen simultaneously. You can get to know Mark and John, for example, through prayerful reading, and as you study these gospels you may easily move from study to prayer and from prayer to study. Your learning enriches your prayer, and your prayer leads to further study. In this book, nevertheless, I must treat these three activities separately, since their goals and methods remain distinct.

I have chosen to include the gospels of Mark and John in the same book because, though similar in their basic story, each gospel tells that story in its own way. Each gospel offers you a distinctive portrait of Jesus' life, death, and resurrection. In the Epilogue I will reflect on some significant differences between

Mark and John and on how their complementary stories can accompany you through life.

I offer this book to you as an approach to Mark and John, and I invite you to use it as freely as you use the gospels themselves. You may be initially drawn to the suggestions for getting to know Mark and John, to the cases and methods for prayer, or to the information about the worlds behind and the story of each gospel. However you use this book, I am convinced that you will ultimately engage in all three activities: that studying these gospels will lead you to prayer, and that praying with them will awaken in you a desire to study them. If this book stimulates and sustains you in these activities it will have accomplished the purpose for which it was written.

I

MARK

1

Getting to Know Mark's Gospel

Mark as "Gospel"

A narrative is an account, a tale, a story, with a setting, characters, and dramatic movement. Mark's account is a narrative; but it is also a "gospel," that is, a proclamation of the Good News, an announcement of God's saving activity in Jesus of Nazareth, an announcement of the coming of God's Kingdom.

Mark pioneered the gospel form for the community of Christians to which he belonged—a mixed community of Gentile and Jewish members. Three elements came together to create Mark's gospel: earlier traditions about Jesus' words and deeds, the Jewish and Greek cultural and religious milieu of the first century A.D., and Mark's own experience within his community. The following diagram gives some sense of that dynamic process:

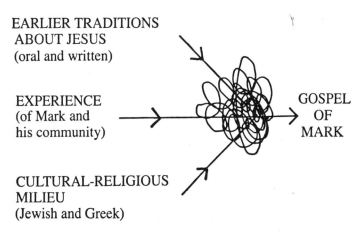

EARLIER TRADITIONS
ABOUT JESUS
(oral and written)

EXPERIENCE
(of Mark and
his community)

GOSPEL
OF
MARK

CULTURAL-RELIGIOUS
MILIEU
(Jewish and Greek)

These three elements interacted with and reshaped one another to finally become the text we call the gospel of Mark.

Though the gospel takes the form of a narrative or story, it is not an exhaustive record of Jesus' words and deeds destined for some historical archive. As narrative, Mark's gospel is a collection of stories about Jesus' words and sayings that have been selected and arranged in a framework of time and place.

To enter into the gospel of Mark, we need first to recognize that the gospel is, was, and always will be a narrative, a story, a tale. Once produced as a written text, Mark's gospel began to have a life of its own. As with any narrative, the gospel was read and reread in settings very different from the original setting of the evangelist and his community. But in this long and varied process, the gospel of Mark has remained a story about Jesus.

Getting to know Mark, then, means learning how to approach the gospel as narrative, learning how to interact with it as a story. I will discuss three elements in Mark that will, I believe, help position you to read the gospel as a story: scenes and sequence, characters and their development, and key episodes.

Scenes and sequence

Mark's gospel can be described as a collection of short, quick scenes that rapidly unfold the story episode by episode. As in a novel or a short story, the scenes are put together with discernible time and/or space intervals between them. For example, when Jesus begins his public ministry in Galilee, the reader follows his movements from place to place and can easily identify the time or space intervals between episodes.

Now after John was arrested,
Jesus came into Galilee. . . .(1:14)

And passing along by the sea of Galilee. . . .(1:16)

And they went into Capernaum;
and immediately on the sabbath he entered the
    synagogue. . . .(1:21)

And immediately. . . .(1:23)

That evening, at sundown. . . .(1:32)

And in the morning, a great while before
    day. . . .(1:35)

And he went throughout all Galilee. . . .(1:39)

Spatial and temporal continuity creates *a sequence of scenes* which discloses an important theme. For example, on the sabbath Jesus demonstrates his power by teaching with authority in the synagogue (1:22), by freeing a man with an unclean spirit (1:23-28), and by healing Simon's mother-in-law (1:29-31). That same evening he frees and heals all who were sick or possessed with demons (1:32-34). These scenes, put together on the same sabbath and with the movement from particular to general exorcisms and healings, suggest that the sequence be called "a day of victories," a positive beginning for Jesus' public ministry.

One of the most striking sequences in Mark is a journey during which Jesus calms the storm at sea (4:35-41), confronts the Gerasene maniac on the other side of the sea (5:1-20), and returns to raise the daughter of Jairus and heal the woman with the issue of blood (5:21-43). These scenes demonstrate how God's power in Jesus conquers the power of evil in its various forms—natural catastrophe, diabolical possession, sickness, and death. Again precise references to time and place weave the scenes into one coherent and dramatic sequence:

On that day, when evening had come,
he said to them,
"Let us go across to the other side."
And leaving the crowd,
they took him with them,
just as he was, in the boat.
And other boats were with him. . . .(4:35-36)

They came to the other side of the sea,
to the country of the Gerasenes. (5:1)

And when Jesus had crossed again in the boat
to the other side, a great crowd gathered
about him; and he was beside the sea. (5:21)

As a last example of scenes building in sequence, we look at Mark's story of the journey from Galilee to Jerusalem (8:27—

10:52). Here the scenes flow episode by episode, building a momentum that carries the reader along. The oft-repeated phrase "on the way" (8:27; 9:33; 10:17; 10:32; 10:52) creates and sustains the image of a journey, and specific references to place inform the readers that Jesus and his followers start out from Caesarea Philippi in the north (8:27), pass through Galilee (9:30), Capernaum (9:33), Judaea and beyond the Jordan (10:1), and Jericho (10:46). The journey sequence ends with Jesus and his followers entering Jerusalem and the Temple (11:11). Through these few examples, we see that clear references to time and place enable us to visualize and experience the gospel's movement.

Elsewhere in Mark, scenes are put together without much concern for temporal or spatial connection. You may feel frustrated and disoriented, since the evangelist is not always as concerned as modern storytellers to show how episodes follow one another. In general, however, by attending to the temporal and spatial framework you will experience the story's fast-moving pace.

Characters and their development

Mark also creates *characters*. The principal character, the one with whom Mark is most interested, is, of course, Jesus of Nazareth. Those with whom Jesus interacts can be grouped as followers, crowds, and Jewish religious authorities. The network of interactions can be visualized in this scheme:

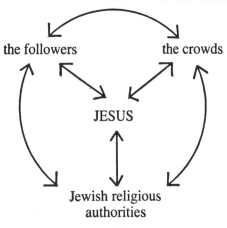

the followers   the crowds

JESUS

Jewish religious
authorities

Followers included all those who follow Jesus—the disciples, the Twelve, Peter, the women. The *crowds* around Jesus are those who respond with enthusiasm to his words and actions but do not commit themselves to follow him. The *Jewish religious authorities* include those from the various movements within Judaism who were openly hostile to Jesus and his followers—the Pharisees, the scribes, the Herodians, the Sadducees, the chief priests, the elders, and the high priest. A fruitful focus in reading Mark's narrative is to watch the interactions between these characters and Jesus, attending to whether and how they change and develop as the story unfolds. We will study characterization more closely after gaining an initial familiarity with the total gospel.

Key episodes

Four pivotal episodes advance the story and build toward answering the central question in Mark's gospel: Who is Jesus?

First, in Mark's gospel Jesus is introduced to us but not to the disciples as "Jesus Christ the Son of God" (1:1). We next meet Jesus at his baptism, as he is empowered by the Spirit to reveal the Kingdom of God and so to confront and destroy the power of evil (1:9-13). The rest of the gospel, episode by episode, shows Jesus gradually revealing to his followers what we, the readers, already know.

In the second pivotal episode, at Caesarea Philippi, Peter professes that Jesus is the Christ, but he fails to understand that Jesus' messiahship must entail suffering, death, and resurrection (8:29, 32b-33).

In the third pivotal episode, the trial scene, the Jewish high priest confronts Jesus, and for the first time Jesus admits in public that he is "the Christ, the Son of the Blessed." Jesus then goes on to speak of himself as the triumphant Son of Man who will sit at the right hand of power and come on the clouds of heaven. The high priest accuses him of blasphemy, and the Jewish authorities condemn him to death (14:60-65).

Finally, at Jesus' death, the pagan centurion makes a strong profession of faith, "Truly this man was the son of God" (15:39). The title that Mark revealed to the reader in the introduction,

Son of God, is now professed not by the Jewish authorities, nor by the Jewish crowds, nor by a follower, but by a pagan, Gentile soldier.

Using these four pivotal episodes, we might visualize the dramatic movement in Mark's narrative as an upward movement from Jesus' baptism to the centurion's profession at the foot of the cross:

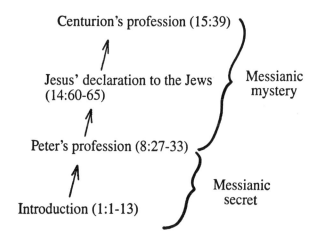

The movement from the introduction to Peter's profession has been entitled "the messianic secret" because within it Jesus reveals by his preaching, teaching, and healing that he is the promised Messiah. But Jesus commands that those who recognize him not tell anyone, since he does not intend to meet the popular Jewish expectation of a national leader dedicated to political and military action against Rome. The movement from Peter's profession to Jesus' declaration and to the centurion's profession has been called "the messianic mystery" because within it Jesus announces the paradox that as Son of Man and Messiah he must first suffer, die, and then be raised in glory—a mystery his followers were unable to comprehend. Reading Mark with attention to these pivotal episodes can put you in touch with this important theme and enable you to watch it unfold.

Reading Mark

I have reflected on the text of Mark as "gospel" and as narrative consisting of scenes and sequence, character, and key episodes. In doing so, I have attempted to create an environment to enable you to interact with the narrative. Now let what I have said fade into the background, and give your full attention to the story itself, allowing it to wash over and through you, listening and receiving it with reverence.

I suggest that you first read Mark in one sitting from beginning to end. Focus your attention on the individual words, phrases, and sentences. This focus will enable you to become more aware of each element in the story. Allow several days or weeks to pass, and again read Mark from beginning to end. This time, focus on sense lines, units of thought, scenes and sequences. Attend to the feel of the story, whether it is hard or soft, warm or cold, appealing or repelling. At a later time, as you read Mark a third time, attend to the feelings that surface as you grow more familiar with the gospel.

After you have completed the three readings, try to find words for your experience of Mark by doing the following exercise:

1. Select at least three adjectives to complete each of the following sentences, and for each adjective indicate passages in Mark that support your choice.

    Mark's gospel is _____, _____, and _____.
    Mark's Jesus is _____, _____, and _____.
    The relationship between Mark's Jesus and his followers
       is _____, _____, and _____.
    The relationship between Mark's Jesus and the Jewish
       authorities is _____, _____, and _____.

2. Think about your response to Mark, and answer these questions:

    What aspects of Mark did you like most?
    What did you find especially meaningful in Mark?
    What aspects of Mark did you ignore?
    What was your overall reaction to Mark?

2

Praying with Mark

Reflections on Prayer

In Chapter 1 you came to know the gospel of Mark by reading it several times and by reflecting on how you reacted to its story of Jesus. In this chapter we will reflect on what it means to pray, especially to pray with the gospel. We will then look at three true-to-life persons who pray with the gospel of Mark. Lastly, we will explain the methods these persons used and suggest how to adapt and use those methods in your own prayer.

The word *prayer* evokes different images: We say formal prayers such as grace at meals and morning or night prayers; we pray together in church on Sundays or at devotions; we pray privately at home or in church; we find God in a beautiful sunrise or in the roaring sea; as we drive to work or home from the supermarket, we reflect on God's action in our everyday lives. We use many styles in our prayer, and we pray at any time, in any place.

However varied the time and place, all prayer is a means for us to know and meet God. Prayer is an encounter with God in love. As such, prayer resembles the encounters in love that occur in a home and create life in a family—encounters between husband and wife, parents and children, and children with one another. As family members reach out in many different ways, they share their lives with one another. How they speak and respond—the quality of their encounters—influences the quality of love in their home.

Our prayer arises from the belief that God wants to reach out and speak to us, that God wants to share his life with us, that God invites us to respond. God's call begins the prayer, but without our response, prayer cannot become an encounter in love between God and ourselves. Not even God can communicate with a spiritually deaf and mute person. So in prayer God reaches out to us, and we try to listen and respond.

How we listen and respond influences the quality of our relationship to God. Prayer is *the* way we communicate and deepen that relationship. Husbands and wives do not marry simply to communicate with each other. But they do not grow in their marriage unless they learn to communicate and attend to the quality of their communication. Though not an end in itself, communication serves their relationship of shared love and intimacy. Similarly, communication in prayer serves our encounter with God. It can take different forms, occur at different times and in different places. But without communication our relationship with God soon deteriorates.

Prayer, like any other encounter in love, demands that we spend focused time with God. Imagine the following scene in a family with five children of grade or high school age. As the children come home for dinner and their father pulls up from work, a certain chaos fills the home. Parents and children interact with one another, and everyone has time for everyone. At the dinner table all share in one floating conversation. But after the dishes, the father invites his third-eldest son to show him the report card that came in the morning mail. Moving to a corner of the house, the father and son forget everyone else and begin to talk about the achievements and disappointments reflected in the son's grades. Their focused time together strengthens their relationship. Similar time with each family member strengthens the entire family network.

We must also spend focused time with God. Though we believe that God is present and active everywhere and in all things, that God is in the world and the world is in God, and that God is the climate in which we live and move and have our being, we need to find time in our busy lives to be alone with God in prayer. We need to set aside all other concerns and give God our best available attention.

Entering into focused time with God involves ritual activity. Again, drawing from our own experiences of human relationships, we can readily see that we have rituals for coming into the presence of another. Less formal, everyday encounters include rituals of preparation. These are, of course more casual, and because the other is a friend or acquaintance, we are able to move quickly into conversation and/or work. But let us imagine that you have decided to make an appointment with a doctor—a more formal encounter, in which you more carefully attend to ritual behavior. You first call the doctor's office to set a definite time for a consultation and to indicate in a general way your reasons for making the appointment. When you arrive at the doctor's office, you may quickly run a comb through your hair; then you walk in and greet the receptionist, who invites you to take a seat. Shortly, a nurse ushers you into a small examination room and routinely takes your temperature, pulse, and blood pressure. When the doctor enters, you engage in light conversation before settling into the examination, prognosis, and prescribed treatment. As the time for your appointment draws to a close, the doctor indicates whether or not you need a future appointment. With a few ritual pleasantries, you wish each other well and prepare to leave the examination office.

Rituals of preparation are also natural when we encounter God in prayer. We first choose the best setting for focused time with God, a place where we can be uninhibited in our response to the Lord and to the work of the Spirit. We then determine the gift we will ask for in our prayer—greater union with God, enlightenment on a particular situation, help for ourselves or others in a time of stress, compassion for the sufferings of people we do not know, stillness and rest in the awareness of God's presence. We next select and prepare a passage from scripture or from some other material that will dispose us for the gift we desire. We then decide how to approach our prayer. Our approach will vary according to the time of day, the passage we have chosen, our mood.

Your willingness to follow and adapt a ritual for prayer expresses your desire for focused time with the Lord, your desire to listen to his word and to respond to him. The following ritual will help you place yourself in God's presence:

> In faith, offer yourself to the Lord and assume the position
> that best helps you become aware of the Lord's presence.

Then with body relaxed, listen to the sounds around you; become conscious of the chair or the floor holding you. . . .

Gradually let go, relaxing the muscles throughout your body. . . . You still hear the sounds around you and feel the air against your skin. Let go of these sounds; let go of the feel of the air around you. Relax and become attentive to the Lord, and respond to his presence.

Your response at this point may become your whole prayer. It may lead into something different from what you had prepared. Your response to the Lord's presence may lead to your asking for the special gift you want from this prayer; it may lead you to the scripture passage you had prepared. Feel free to move when your prayer leads you and to remain when your prayer brings you to rest.

At the heart of prayer is the art of listening and responding. Some find it hard to listen to others. We seem to hear but not understand what they are saying. Our ears pick up sounds, but our hearts do not seem to attend to their meaning. But when we really communicate with another person, we first try to listen and then to respond. As we grow in our ability to listen and respond, we enter more deeply into the relationship. Similarly, in our prayer we first listen for God to speak with or without words, and then we respond with head and heart. As we grow in our ability to listen and respond to God in prayer, we enter more deeply into relationship with him.

When we use scripture for prayer, we approach the biblical text in faith. That is, we believe that God wants to communicate with us and encounter us in and through his word, and that the risen Lord wants to establish and maintain a personal relationship with us through the stories about his life, death, and resurrection. With the eyes of faith, we see scripture as the inspired word of God, as a privileged place to encounter God and the risen Lord, as a means God has chosen to communicate with us and to deepen our relationship with him.

In praying with scripture we also listen actively to the text. But since a text cannot speak for itself, we must give it a voice by using our minds to ask questions about this particular scene or by using our imaginations to see the persons, hear their words, and watch their actions. As we listen to the text, we remain attentive to the God who wishes to encounter us in and through his inspired word.

We approach the gospel of Mark in prayer, not to learn about the gospel, but to meet the risen Lord and come to know, love, and serve him: "to see him more clearly, love him more dearly, and follow him more nearly day by day." We believe that Jesus is risen from the dead and sits at the right hand of the Father. We are convinced that by praying with Mark's gospel we will be invited into relationship with the Lord as he lives today in glory.

The gospel serves as a springboard for prayer. The text opens to the risen Lord. The gospel resembles a curtain at a stage play: As we wait for the play to begin, we sit and look at the curtain. But once it opens, we relate to the actors' words and actions. Similarly, we attend to the stories and sayings in the gospel only until they open up to an encounter with the risen Lord. Gradually, the stories of our own lives interact with Mark's story of Jesus' life, death, and resurrection. Jesus begins to become real to us, and we experience ourselves being drawn toward him. We listen and respond. In this way, Mark's gospel or any other scripture text is a means for the risen Lord to communicate with us and invite us to encounter him in love.

No one can predict or control the outcome of prayer. At times we may be aware of feeling strongly and deeply connected to the Lord, and we want to say: "Lord, I believe. . . . Lord, it is good to know you. . . . I trust you. . . . Teach me to trust you more. . . . Lord, you really love me. . . . And I really love you."

At other times we may feel a deep sense of inner peace, even when on the surface our lives seem chaotic. Though we allow ourselves to become involved in too many activities, we have a sense that we are not alone in our journey, that God travels with us through all the chaos. We know that we remain in good relationship with God, and that knowledge gives us deep peace and joy. We thank God for the awareness that we are finding ourselves and him at a level deeper than the good feelings and sensible consolation we may have experienced previously.

At still other times it may seem as though we are making no progress in our prayer. The gospel texts are boring, and the time we spend in prayer seems an eternity. Praying with Mark's gospel becomes hard work accompanied by endless distractions. Prayer has lost all attraction and seems a total waste of time. We begin to feel discouraged because we feel that we pray less well than we used to. At such times we might well recall that we do not come to prayer so that something will happen; rather, we come to spend time with the risen Lord. The sign of true prayer is not how we feel but our willingness, no matter how we feel, to spend focused time with the Lord. When nothing seems to happen in prayer, we do well to recall that our relationship with the Lord often grows more because we have simply spent the time with him; our relationship with God cannot be gauged by what or how we feel during our prayers. Surprisingly, as we leave such prayer to move quietly through the day, we are often aware that even though our prayer did not yield a good feeling, it did express our desire to know the risen Lord and let him lead and guide us on our journey.

Prayer has meaning if we have somehow touched that deepest desire to know and love God, to be known and loved by God, to encounter God in our lives. We come to recognize that this desire is from God and that he wants to speak to us and communicate with us more than we want to listen or respond to him. God gives us the desire to pray and calls us to prayer. God invites us into relationship with him and enables us to respond to his invitation. Dialogue in prayer is not something we achieve by our own efforts. It is all gift. We are gifted to want to pray, gifted with God's invitation to pray, and gifted freely to answer his invitation. Gratitude, then, is a basic attitude in prayer, a gratitude based on faith, a gratitude that quiets us and opens us to the reality of God in our lives.

We will now explore three methods for praying with Mark: "simple reading," "sacred reading," and "imaginative contemplation." All three methods presume that we are endowed with minds to think about a scripture text and with imaginations to dream, fantasize, and feel deeply about what the text discloses. Both mind and imagination are involved in coming to know God in prayer. When we are more inclined to think and reason than to use our imaginations, "sacred reading" will appeal more as a method for praying with scripture. We will find "imaginative contemplation" a more appealing method when we wish to participate in the stories through imagination. Keep in mind, though, that we each blend mind and imagination in the method that best serves our prayer. As our prayer changes, that blend will also change.

In exploring each method, we will first describe a person's experience in using it for prayer, then reflect on the person's experience, and finally describe how you can use the method. Though we will discuss the methods in the context of praying with Mark, we can use them with any biblical writing. Methods for praying with scripture are never tied to a particular biblical writing, but the three methods we have chosen here are especially well suited to Mark's story of Jesus, with its rapid movement and vivid episodes.

Cases and Methods

Simple reading

Lucy is a woman in her forties. She is married and has four sons. She works full-time as a registered nurse. Lucy's need for counseling and spiritual direction became evident when her husband went into treatment for alcohol dependency. Lucy also began the co-dependency treatment, and gradually she came to see how she also had abused alcohol. After work Lucy would drink to keep functioning, since it mellowed her out and gave her enough calm to get through the evening. Her relationship with her husband had badly deteriorated. The entire family was upset, and money problems complicated an already-tense situation. Nothing seemed to be working, and home was anything but a fun place to be.

When Lucy began her treatment, she at first experienced great difficulty admitting that she was unable to manage her use of alcohol, and she was frightened when she realized that in abusing alcohol, she had also abused the people she loved most. She felt a deep sense of shame and guilt for the hurt that she had caused others and herself, but she also felt hopeful that life could be different for her and her family. On the last day of her treatment, while doing the post-treatment life-plan, Lucy's counselor said, "Remember, this is also a spiritual program. In addition to meeting regularly with support groups, you must take quiet time each day to turn your life over to God."

Lucy attended AA meetings, and she also contacted a spiritual director for help in her spiritual program. She was convinced that quiet time with God was an important part of her continuing recovery. She was worried that without it she would start drinking again. She described for her director how she used her quiet time: "When I sit down for my quiet time, I experience mixed emotions. I recycle my shame, and I don't know what I'm doing with the time. I have read *Alcoholics Anonymous: Twelve Steps and Twelve Traditions, Twenty-four Hours a Day,* my Al-Anon book, and a devotional pamphlet. And I make resolutions. I do all that, but I don't feel quiet. I feel disconnected from God and religion. And at the end of my quiet time I'm more stirred up and busy than quiet."

Lucy's director pointed out that her recovery from alcoholism involved learning how to be with the people she loved most. Alcohol had helped her merely exist with her family in the same house, but now as the weeks went by she was learning to be with them and live with them simply as a wife and mother. She and her husband were rediscovering their love, learning how to be with each other in more life-giving ways, and were reaffirming their desire to spend the rest of their lives together. She also began to see that she needed to find quiet ways of being with God in a place where she thought God would talk to her, be with her, and strengthen her in her daily life.

Lucy began to set aside some focused time for herself and God. Her director suggested that instead of trying to figure out what she was going to do with her life, she just read the scriptures—specifically, the gospel of Mark: "Read Mark! Read the whole story as a story. Remember how you told me your story and described some incidents that led to your current problems? Could you read the gospel as though Mark were telling you a story about someone important to him, Jesus of Nazareth, someone he'd like you to get to know, someone you already want to know so that your life will be different? Would you be able to read Mark's gospel the way you read a story, or a collection of stories, or the recollection of a man who loved Jesus very much and wanted to share him with you?"

Lucy read Mark's story of Jesus three or four times. She read it as though the writer were talking to her about a close personal friend. She began to sense the difference Jesus made in people's lives and could make in her life. In the evening, she picked up the gospel instead of a magazine. She read Mark simply as a story about Jesus.

Later she went through the gospel paragraph by paragraph, scene by scene, praying that she might hear Jesus tell her about himself in and through each scene. She asked to believe that the Lord wanted to speak more than she wanted to listen. As Lucy read Mark one paragraph at a time, she attended to the text, but she also listened for Jesus. She asked the Jesus in each healing story to help her let go of her shame, to help her stop trying to "fix" her family; she asked him to bring healing to herself, her husband, and their children.

She recognized that Jesus took a long time instructing his chosen disciples and that in spite of their misunderstandings, he never went back on that choice nor disassociated himself from his followers. Lucy realized that in her baptism the same Lord had chosen her, and she began to sense that he would not go back on that choice either, would not separate himself from her. She could leave him, but she could not make him stop loving her. "When I get scared and feel ashamed, I know I can turn to Jesus, who is always so careful in healing and teaching people. I can turn to him and say, 'You'll never leave me no matter what I do'."

A month later she told her director that she used to hate admitting she was powerless, but now she was beginning to celebrate her weakness. Now she could tell Jesus how she still finds it hard to let go of such things as fighting with her husband and worrying too much. She could also share with him her personal victories—the times when she did succeed in letting go. In a word, the Jesus whom Lucy encountered in Mark's gospel was someone with whom she could talk about what really mattered. Lucy still reads Mark as the story of Jesus. Because she knows the story and has come to know him in the story, she can talk to Jesus out of the positive and negative experiences of her life. In this sharing of stories, Lucy encountered Jesus in love.

As we reflect on this account, we can see how Lucy's life story connected with Mark's story about Jesus. As she read about Jesus healing the sick and possessed, she touched her own need and her family's need for personal healing. She gradually asked Jesus to show her the same compassion that he showed the blind and the lame, the sick and the possessed. She also began to experience how she resembled Jesus' followers in their infidelity and lack of understanding. Lucy now had real hope that Jesus would remain as faithful to her as he had to them.

As Lucy let herself be drawn into Mark's stories about Jesus, they gradually led her to encounter the risen Lord. As the stories touched her need for greater stability and security, Jesus began to become real to her. Lucy began to experience herself relating to him in her daily life. Mark's stories were the means through which Jesus made himself known to her and through which she began to listen to him and to respond in prayer.

Lucy was comfortable with the method of "simple reading," because it was especially well suited to her at this time in her life. She had been trying to *do* prayer in the hope that it would provide an instant and infallible cure for her problems with her husband and family. She had been filling her prayer with slogans and needless complications. What Lucy needed was a simple approach as an antidote to her compulsive nature. Simply reading Mark proved an effective means for her to encounter the Lord.

The golden rule for this method of praying scripture is to keep it simple. Avoid approaching prayer as a task; try not to analyze the text or to apply it to your life. For five or ten minutes a day, simply read Mark's gospel the way you would read a story, a collection of stories or the rememberings of a man who loved Jesus Christ and wanted to share him with you. Let yourself be given the story as a story. As you read, stop when you find yourself drawn to certain elements in the story, when you find something meaningful, or when you experience resistance to the story. Let the text open up to you; listen to it and through it to the risen Lord. Then respond by talking to Jesus from your life situation. Gradually you will experience resemblances between the stories in Mark and your own story—between the healings and your need to be healed, between Jesus' relation to his followers and your desire for such closeness, between the disciples' misunderstanding and your own, between Jesus' passage through death to glory and your experiences of apparently meaningless sufferings. As the stories in Mark gradually become your stories and as these resemblances become clear, you will begin to encounter the risen Lord. As you move into a closer relationship with him, focus on listening and responding to him. Attend to Mark's gospel only as it continues to serve your encounter with the Lord.

Sacred reading *(lectio divina)*

Marie, a single woman in her thirties and from a middle-class family, was educated in a private Eastern school. Her family church background was Episcopalian. She made her first communion and was confirmed in that church. When she reflected on her church membership she said, "It was a society church. I went to that church because my family went. It felt stiff and formal, but my going pleased my parents."

In college Marie stopped attending church. After college she began a successful teaching career. Her income enabled her to accumulate a car, a house, and elegant clothes, and to go on expensive vacations. She described her life as "my-centered— my house, my clothes, my social life." She also had an affair that lasted four years. After ending it, she experienced life as empty and dissatisfying.

At thirty-one, Marie left teaching to work in an insurance office. There she met a young woman who told Marie about her own efforts to build self-confidence and about what belonging to a church meant to her. The woman said that without religion and God she would never have survived a messy divorce. Marie was fascinated; she began to shop for a church and joined a Congregational church. Many of the people there seemed to be like her—disaffected from and disenchanted with Christianity. Nonetheless, the church was a good place for considering reentry into the Christian faith. Marie found the highly intellectual sermons both stimulating and satisfying. But she also envied her friend at the office who seemed to have more than intellectual answers to life's problems.

Her friend brought Marie to a self-help seminar where she heard one of the speakers say: "The gospels say the same thing as self-help psychology, namely, that when we recognize our basic beauty and goodness, we are claiming what is real and true about humans. Without denying our brokenness, we see that we can be loved and loving persons." Marie was strongly attracted to this idea, but she was also frightened. Later she became aware that she wanted some answers, that she was searching deeply for a sense of belonging, and that she was on a journey toward God. Once aware of her search for God, Marie returned to the question "What is a gospel? What does it say?" She responded with the textbook answers she had learned as a student.

She started talking to her friend at the office about a most important personal issue: that she was single and felt dissatisfaction at not being married. She said, "Something must be wrong with me. If I were married, I'd have a wonderful life. I'd know that I'm lovable."

Marie tried to describe to her friend her experience of prayer. She remembered panic prayers and night prayers as a child with her parents. But the word "prayer" had little meaning for her. She had almost no image of interpersonal, I-Thou prayer. Her friend asked Marie whether instead of studying the gospels, she would like to pray with the gospel of Mark. The suggestion appealed to Marie, even though she had no sense of how to use a gospel for prayer. Her friend stressed the importance of approaching Mark with faith and an open heart. She asked Marie where she thought God wanted to meet her in her life, and urged her to ask God to communicate with her.

Marie began to pray with Mark's gospel. She grew accustomed to finding a good time for prayer and of taking time to quiet herself and enter the prayer. Then she would select a scene from Mark like the cure of the paralytic (2:1-12) and would read it slowly and attentively at least three times, sometimes aloud so she could hear as well as see the words. She became as present to the passage as possible, letting it enter her whole person.

Next she began to think about the passage and try to understand its message. She reflected on questions like the following: What is the action? Why is it going on? What is the physical setting? What is the time setting? Who are the persons in the scene? Who does what and why? Who speaks? What happens in response? With whom do I most identify? What is the central element in the scene?

Gradually, Marie began to react to what the scene said to her, what questions it raised, what she liked and didn't like, the places where she wanted to tell Jesus to act or respond differently. She reflected on what struck her and how it struck her. Marie was gradually drawn to ask what all this had to do with her life. She looked for resemblances between the action in the story and the action in her own life story. She wondered what those resemblances might mean in terms of God revealing himself to her. She found herself able to look at Jesus in the story, and she began to discuss these questions with him. She tried to talk to him about the resemblances she saw between her life and his care for the paralytic. She was touched by the intimate relationship between Jesus and the four men who brought their friend for healing. They were convinced that Jesus could heal their friend, and they expressed that conviction in action. They climbed the stairway outside the crowded house, dug a hole in the mud-and-straw roof and lowered their friend to Jesus' feet. Jesus dealt quickly with the paralyzed man and used his power to cure his disease. Later, Marie wrote of her experiences of praying with the gospel: "Finding out that scripture could really apply to my life and speak to me now, I began to know the wonder of seeing old tales become current. I'm amazed that instead of being dry and dead, Mark's gospel is alive and life-giving."

Marie began to reflect on how she felt about marriage. She named the fact that she was running from dissatisfaction and that she imagined marriage would solve everything. She began to look at her earlier affair and she saw in it almost no communication or mutuality. Marie began to realize her deep desire for intimacy. Jesus' actions with the paralytic led her to ask, "Is intimacy with Jesus Christ a real possibility for me? If not, what will intimacy be in my life?" She began to talk with the Lord about intimacy, about how he loved people as they are, even when he challenged them. Marie gradually found herself saying, "I want to know Jesus Christ. I dare to believe that Jesus Christ can be the center of my life."

Marie moved slowly into dialogue with Jesus, a style of prayer she had formerly considered "nonsense" piety. As she talked, she grew quietly aware that she could count on Jesus being there for her in her life—at the office, in her relationships, and in her time alone. She grew more and more comfortable with dialogue prayer, and she began to use it outside the focused time of prayer. As she met the demands of her job, she would find herself talking to Jesus. She would tell him what she was doing and share with him what was on her mind. As she encountered the Lord she had once hoped to meet, she moved from fascination at praying with Mark to fascination with Jesus Christ.

Where did Marie's life intersect with the story of the paralytic? In her journey in and out of Christian churches and self-help groups, Marie's search for a sense of belonging had been left unsatisfied. As she thought about the men bringing their paralytic friend to Jesus, she began to realize that her search had been for Jesus, who was someone with whom she could be intimate. Marie also grew aware of her unsolved feelings about marriage. When she saw how Jesus cared for the paralytic and his friends, she realized that he would care for her and invite her to share her life with him.

Marie found "sacred reading" a comfortable method for praying with Mark. At first she had followed a more intellectual approach to Christianity, one that could satisfy her mind and answer her questions. Through her friend at the office, she later began to see that intellectual answers alone would not fill her desire for God. She began to search for a total human experience in prayer, an experience that would nourish both mind and heart. "Sacred reading," with its movement from reading to thinking and from thinking to a personal encounter with the Lord, was in harmony with Marie's inner movement.

You too may find "sacred reading" *(lectio divina)* a good method for praying with scripture. After preparing for prayer and putting yourself in God's presence, *read* the passage from scripture. In a slow, meditative reading, dwell on each element in the text. Read the passage several times, out loud if possible, until something draws you or repels you. At that point, begin to *meditate,* that is, to reason about what has awakened your mind and heart. Ask questions about what the passage might mean. What is the action? Why is it going on? What is the physical setting? What is the time setting? Who are the persons in the scene? Who does what, and why? Who speaks? What happens in response? With whom do I most identify? What is the central element in the scene?

As you think and reason about the text, you may begin to sense resemblances between the scene and your life experiences. You may notice what Jesus reveals about himself both in the text and in your experience, and you may begin to move into dialogue with Jesus in *prayer.* Speak spontaneously to the Lord, or remain silent in his presence. Close the scripture, shut your eyes, and open your heart to this encounter in love with the Lord. Remain in prayer as long as you are not too distracted. When distractions make prayer difficult, read the scripture again and move from reading to meditation and from meditation to prayer.

Prayer is much more to be experienced than described. It is a pure gift, granted when, how, and to the extent the Lord wishes to grant it. You can only know of such prayer and believe in it, hope for and desire it, and wait for it with patience.

"Sacred reading" differs from "simple reading." In "sacred reading," you select one passage, think and reason about particular elements in the passage, and move from reading through meditation to prayer. In using "simple reading" as a method, you read Mark as a story; you do not meditate on a passage, nor do you think about how it applies to your life. You simply let yourself be given the story as a story. In "simple reading" avoid meditation, which is the key activity in "sacred reading."

"Sacred reading" is an excellent form of prayer for people like Marie who want to pray more with the heart (affect) than with the mind (intellect). "Sacred reading" enables you to participate in meditation with your intellect, but it gently moves you from thinking to affective prayer. This method can help you discover how the gospel can touch your life. Through it you may also learn to trust your imagination and may begin to risk a more imaginative style of contemplation.

Imaginative contemplation

Steve came from a small Southern town. Since his father was a professional army officer, Steve had grown up in many different countries. After college and some work experience, Steve joined the army during the Vietnam war. He questioned the rightness of the United States' involvement, but he also saw personal advantages to enlisting. He was at a transition time in his life, and by enlisting he could avoid small-town and family pressures about his plans for the future. With compulsory military service behind him, Steve would be free to decide his own future. When he enlisted, he chose to go to Vietnam rather than to enter officer's training school and follow his father's career.

As an infantryman in Vietnam, Steve witnessed events that horrified and upset him—children dreadfully dismembered, little towns ravished, small farms burnt out, and rice fields sprayed with poisonous chemicals. He watched men he knew change into ruthless killers, and he soon realized he simply could no longer point a gun and pull the trigger.

Steve had an opportunity to join the Green Berets, and he took it. As a member of the Green Berets, his duty time was cut in half. Steve became a medic and worked with the advance line units. He picked up the wounded and rushed them to nearby stations. Many would never again be able to lead normal lives: some were dreadfully shell-shocked; some men's minds had snapped; some would be patched up and returned to the front lines. These scenes tore at Steve's heart, and he began to experience a strong sense of futility and helplessness. He just wanted to finish his time, return to marry the woman he loved, and start a home.

As often as he could, Steve attended the field worship service. He was not a very religious man, but he was sensitive and deeply feeling. He had compassion for the injured men, and his participation in their lives made it all the more painful to remain in Vietnam. The worship service was an oasis in the desert of brutality, a calm harbor in a storm of destruction.

One Sunday, the presiding minister read and preached on Mark's account of Jesus healing the paralytic (Mk 2:1-12). He read the story with such feeling that Steve's attention was drawn away from all other concerns. He entered the story. The minister invited the soldiers to reconstruct the scene in their imagination. Capernaum was like the little towns around them in Vietnam. Crowds were moving toward the house in the center of town where they hoped to see a man named Jesus, who supposedly had power to heal the sick and wounded. Steve mingled with the people and walked with them to the house. In their faces he could see the harsh reality of their lives, but also their conviction that Jesus could heal them.

Next the minister invited his congregation to stand with the crowd at the door and feel their needs, needs that were the same in Capernaum and in Vietnam. Four men suddenly realized that they might not get their paralytic friend to Jesus, since it was late in the afternoon. Steve watched them carry their crippled friend up the outside stairs to the roof, dig a hole in the mud-and-straw roof, lower their friend through the hole, and set him down at the feet of Jesus. Jesus responded to their faith: "My son, your sins are forgiven. . . . I say to you, rise, take up your pallet and go home. . . ." The minister concluded by inviting and challenging the soldiers to bring themselves, wounded in body or spirit, to the same Jesus and be ready to hear him respond with the same words.

Later that afternoon, as Steve rested in his bunk, he remained wrapped in the story of the paralytic. It had captured his imagination at the worship service, and it stayed with him. He imagined himself back in the crowd outside the house: With him in a wheelchair was a young infantryman and friend who was severely crippled from the waist down. Steve said: "Maybe I can get you to Jesus. I'll do what I can." As the four men left to climb the stairs with their paralytic friend, Steve decided to push through the crowds. As a medic, he could easily manage the wheelchair. So he put on his medic armband and asked the crowd to clear a path. They stepped aside, and Steve began to push the wheelchair into the house. The chair stopped at the door. Steve had a clear path to Jesus, and he saw him sitting in the inner room. But the chair wouldn't move. Steve pushed, but the chair wouldn't budge. He used all his strength, but he couldn't move the chair. When he asked the people for help, they refused, saying *he* must get the crippled man to Jesus. Steve continued to struggle with the wheelchair, but he failed to push or lift it over the threshhold.

As Steve struggled, he began to sense that neither the wheel-chair nor his disabled friend was the source of the problem. Steve himself was the immovable obstacle. In his heart he was not convinced that once he pushed the crippled man into the house, Jesus would heal him. Vietnam had crippled him with cynicism and doubt. As he continued to struggle with the chair, Steve recalled other futile efforts to heal the horrors of war. He grew increasingly aware that the deep futility inside him was wrestling with a fragile sense of hope. Could Jesus do something for this crippled soldier and for himself? To be convinced that Jesus could heal them, Steve had to give up his futility. He desired to believe and hope in the power of God at work in Jesus' healings, and he asked for the courage to reach out for life, even when death surrounded him. He tried again to push the wheelchair, and it began to move.

Steve brought his friend to Jesus. As the three became present to one another, Steve experienced a deep, wordless, inner healing. He heard Jesus say to his friend: "Your sins are forgiven. . . . Take up your pallet and go home." Steve remained in the Lord's presence until the call to duty interrupted his prayer.

Steve finished out his time in Vietnam no less sensitive to the horrors around him. But since he had begun to choose life in the midst of death, to hope in the face of despair, to see that the power of life can be greater than the power of death, he did not crack under the pressure. He had always been known for his gentle, caring manner, but now he was also seen as a person of hope. His prayer deepened and grew. It didn't provide an escape from Vietnam; but it enabled Steve to live and work more effectively in that death-like situation. When his time ended, Steve returned to the United States. He resumed civilian life with surprising ease, married the woman he loved, and with her bought a home and made plans for a family.

Where did Steve's story merge with Mark's story of the paralytic? Steve was used to serving the sick and the wounded. Because of his frustration at all he had experienced as a medic in Vietnam, he easily identified with the four men in their frustration that they might not get their paralytic friend to Jesus. Once he had cleared a path to Jesus, Steve began, in his imagination, to feel blocked and confused. A deep futility prevented him from wheeling the infantryman to Jesus. The futility about the war infected his belief in humankind, clouded his faith in Jesus. Mark's story of the cure gradually confronted Steve's story of futility and disbelief. Eventually, Steve's story converged with Mark's story. Steve struggled between faith in Jesus' power and doubt that Jesus could do anything at all. He felt challenged to choose life in spite of death and to hope in spite of futility.

Steve's vivid imagination enabled him to participate in Mark's story of the paralytic. Steve had always lived in the movies he saw or the novels he read, so he spontaneously and quite naturally entered into the cure of the paralytic. Steve models for us, especially for those of us with vivid imaginations, how we can enter into and live in Mark's stories about Jesus.

In our culture, movies and TV draw us into human situations. Why do we cry at a sad movie? Surely not because a piece of film is running through a projector or because certain shadows are appearing on the screen. We cry because through our imagination we are participating in the story. Assuming the attitudes of the actors, we live in it. We let their feelings become our feelings.

You can also live in the stories about Jesus through a method of prayer called "imaginative contemplation." Like Steve, let yourself be drawn into a concrete scene from Jesus' earthly life. Listen to the words and watch the actions. Discover more about Jesus, about his world view, about his feelings and values. At the same time, discover more about yourself, about how your story merges or does not merge with his, about how your values and feelings agree or disagree with his. As the two stories interact, you begin to relate more deeply to the risen Lord. The stories melt away as you come to encounter him in love.

How do you use "imaginative contemplation"? First, quiet yourself. Next, take time to let your imagination create the entire setting. Let the scene present itself to you, and present yourself to the scene. What kind of place is it? Clean or dirty? Large or small? Notice the architecture and the weather. In your imagination, create the setting before the actors arrive.

With the stage prepared, the whole scene comes to life. See the persons. How many are there? What sort of persons? How are they dressed? What are they doing? What are they saying? What's behind what they're saying and doing? It is not enough for you to observe the whole scene from the outside: Enter into it. What are you doing there? Why have you come to this place? What are your feelings as you survey the scene and watch these persons? What are you doing? Do you speak to anyone? To whom? About what?

Having positioned yourself in the scene, notice the central characters. Who are they? Where are they? How are they dressed? Is anyone with them? Walk up to them and speak to them. What do you say to them, or what do you ask them? What do they say in reply? Spend time getting as much information about their lives as you can. What impression do they make on you? What do you feel as you converse with them?

As you speak to the characters, notice that Jesus has come. Watch his actions and movements. Where does he go? How does he act? What do you think he is feeling? He now comes toward you and the central characters. What do you feel as he approaches? Perhaps you step aside when you realize he wants to talk to one of the others. What does he say? How does the person respond? Listen to the dialogue, especially to Jesus' instructions. Watch his actions. Notice the other person's reactions, then Jesus' reactions, and especially your own reactions.

Now Jesus turns to speak to you. What does he say? How do you respond? Talk to him about what has taken place and how it relates to your experience. Spend time in prayer, with or without words, in the company of Jesus. This encounter with the risen Lord has been the gift you desired in the contemplation: "to see thee more clearly, love thee more dearly, follow thee more nearly day by day."

As we have mentioned, "imaginative contemplation" may appeal more to persons who find it easy to live in biblical stories through their imagination, whereas "sacred reading" may appeal more to those who prefer to think about and reflect on the same stories. Marie thought about the story of the paralytic, and through her thinking she was drawn into an affective encounter with the Lord. Steve entered the same scene with his feelings and imagination, and through his participation met the same Lord. You may be drawn to one method rather than another because of your temperament, your personal preferences, or your concrete situation. But you must always remember that the methods are valuable not in themselves but as means to encounter Jesus in love.

Prayer with Mark can awaken in you the desire to study the gospel, and studying Mark can enrich your prayer. As you pray with Mark, you may begin to wonder about this gospel's historical background, its portrait of Jesus and the disciples, its dramatic movement, its view of the world. You may want to study Mark, apart from your prayer. Studying Mark can enrich your prayer, and continued prayer can stimulate further study. Through the interaction of personal prayer and study, you can deepen your religious appreciation of this gospel.

3

Historical Background: The World Behind Mark

Since the gospel of Mark that we read today originated in A.D. 70, it naturally reflects a religious milieu that differs from our twentieth-century experience. When we recognize the difference in milieu and the distance in time, we may begin to feel alienated from Mark and to question the appreciation we have begun to enjoy. How can we pray with a text that has come to us from such a distant past and such a different milieu? We can explore the historical setting of the gospel and search out the literal meaning that Mark intended. We can thereby gain a feel for the gospel in its own environment, the world in which it was produced, the world behind the text. We can ask: How did this gospel come to be written? What did Mark and his community experience? What did the written text mean to Mark and his community? What effect did the gospel have on Mark's community?

By seeking answers to these questions, we can reconstruct Mark's situation. Without denying the cultural differences and temporal distance that separate Mark's community from ours, we can discover resemblances between their situation and our own. These resemblances make meaningful dialogue possible between Mark's believing community and ourselves, members of the believing community who read his gospel today. Our desire to understand the gospel of Mark itself in its own world arises from the conviction that this historical reconstruction will ultimately enrich and deepen our religious appreciation and our prayer life.

I have briefly described (in "Getting to Know Mark's Gospel") how these three elements come together to create what we call Mark's gospel—the earlier traditions about Jesus' words and deeds, the cultural-religious milieu of first-century Hellenism and Judaism, and the concrete experience of Mark and his community. Now we will explore the interaction among tradition, culture, and experience.

Prewar Judaism in Palestine

The religion of Judaism, like almost every religion in the Hellenistic Age (from the Greco-Macedonian conqueror Alexander the Great, 323 B.C., to Constantine, who died in A.D. 337), remained a majority religion in Palestine and became a minority religion in foreign cities. For example, the gods and goddesses—Isis of Egypt, Bal of Syria, the Great Mother of Phyrgia, and Mithra of Kurdistan—were worshiped in their native lands as well as in Rome and other cosmopolitan centers. With few exceptions, each of these ancient religious traditions, originally tied to a specific geographical area and people, spread to other lands.

Nationalistic, messianic movements existed within Judaism in Palestine when Jesus lived there. In fact, prior to the tragic revolt against Rome (A.D. 66-70), a war that ended with the destruction of Jerusalem and of the Temple, Judaism embraced different parties and movements. Far from being a monolithic religion with a fixed set of orthodox beliefs and uniform practices, Judaism showed considerable tolerance for varied, even opposed, practices and doctrines. However, Judaism rested on two strong pillars—the Temple worship in Jerusalem and the observance of the Law as found in a more-or-less common scripture. Convictions about the Temple and the Law allowed Judaism to welcome under its large umbrella such diverse groups as the Sadducees, the Essenes, the Pharisees, the Zealots, and the followers of Jesus of Nazareth.

The Sadducees, the priestly and aristocratic bureaucracy of Judaism, were not simply identified with the priesthood. Though many of them belonged to the upper ranks of the priestly hierarchy, Sadducees were also members of the landed aristocracy. They found their orbit around the power based in Jerusalem, where the priestly aristocracy worked to accommodate the Temple and its worship to their non-Jewish political rulers. Though the

Sadducees adapted to political realities, in religious matters they were rigid and conservative traditionalists. Faithful to the original, literal meaning of scripture, they insisted that only the written Law should form the basis for Jewish religious life, and they reacted strongly against any developments in later writings or in further reflection on the Law and its meaning. The Sadducees, practical men of high social standing, ran the affairs of their nation in commonsense fashion, striking the best bargains with their Roman oppressors for both their people and themselves.

The Essenes, who reacted strongly to the political alliance achieved by the Sadducees, formed monastic communities apart from the Temple—communities where they attempted to live in complete fidelity to the Jewish Law. Ruins of such a monastery were discovered in 1947 on the northwest shore of the Dead Sea, near the desert valley of Quamran. The monastery's library of scrolls—the Dead Sea Scrolls, as they have come to be known—give us fascinating insights into the mentality of this breakaway group. The scrolls disclose how the Essenes attempted to live in utmost religious purity while waiting for the genuine priesthood to be restored and the liturgy at the Temple to be purified. This sectarian movement, a priestly and monastic order of Jewish ascetics, opposed, both historically and in principle, the Temple and its sacrificial cult. The Essenes cultivated a strict separateness from people, cities, and the world. Elaborate baptismal rites and sacred meals were central in their religious community, and some form of common ownership seems to have characterized their life together.

The Pharisaic movement, made up of laymen, particularly lay scribes, successfully steered a middle course between the Sadducees' religious compromises and the Essenes' complete withdrawal from Jerusalem and the Temple. Because they refused to take the expedient course, as they perceived the Sadducees to have done, the Pharisees were denied much direct involvement in the religious and political leadership in Palestine. But since they challenged the power of the landed aristocracy and rejected compromise with foreign power, they enjoyed a well-earned respect and influence with the Jewish people. Pharisaism was a movement that could not be ignored, since through their extensive system of oral commentary, the Pharisees attempted to make the Law more livable and within reach of the people. Unlike the Sadducees, the Pharisees were open to development in Jewish thought. They accepted the great network of oral commentary that had grown up around the written Law—commentary which they saw not as a subversion but as an insurance that the Law was still alive and active in people's everyday lives. Pharisaic devotion to the Mosaic Law was, therefore, anything but a blind embrace of legalism and strict adherence to the letter. The Pharisees' adaptability was their strength, since it enabled them to establish a wide power-base in the synagogues throughout Palestine and the diaspora.

The Christian movement, with its predominantly Jewish beginnings in Palestine, understood itself as another sectarian movement under the large umbrella of Judaism. What differentiated Christian Jews from other Jews was the fact that they professed Jesus of Nazareth to be the Messiah. In their worship at the Temple and in their observance of the Law, however, Christian Jews could not be distinguished from the other Jews in Jerusalem.

The earliest description of the Jerusalem community discloses its life within Judaism:

> And all who believed were together and had all things in common; and they sold their possessions and goods and distributed them to all, as any had need. And day by day, attending the temple together and breaking bread in their homes, they partook of food with glad and generous hearts, praising God and having favor with all the people. (Acts 2:44-47)

The Judeo-Christian community in Jerusalem was characterized by strong personal bonds among the members (Acts 4:23—5:16). The twelve apostles linked the Jerusalem community to the earthly Jesus, since they had been chosen by him, had accompanied him from Galilee to Jerusalem, and had witnessed his appearances as their risen Lord. Since Peter, more than the others, provided continuity with Jesus, he played a decisive role in the choice of Matthias in place of Judas Iscariot (Acts 1:15-26) and in the crucial decision made in Jerusalem about admitting Gentiles to the Christian community (Acts 15). Peter was a preacher in the Jerusalem community, a missionary preacher to outsiders, and a spokesman for the community (Acts 2:14-36; 4:8-12; 5:29-32; 10:34-43; 15:7-11). His martyrdom in Rome under Emperor Nero in A.D. 68-69 created a leadership vacuum for Judeo-Christians in Palestine.

First Revolt Against Rome

Activists, who regarded themselves as the zealous agents of God's wrath and the instruments through which God was to deliver his people, emerged as the Zealot movement at the time of the first revolt against Rome (A.D. 66-70), but their brand of radical nationalism may have begun to crystallize during Jesus' own lifetime. Zealots maintained that Jewish independence would be achieved only through military action against the Romans. Roman power did not discourage Zealots, since they firmly believed that if God's people began the struggle, God would intervene to establish his kingdom, the kingdom of Israel.

The Zealots carved out their revolution in stages. A series of abortive attempts to overthrow the Romans in the early decades of the first century prepared for a general uprising triggered under Zealot leadership in A.D. 66. The Jews fought with courage, but like many radical revolutionary movements, they were divided by internal struggles and dissensions. As many as six different groups were deadly enemies to one another. The Roman general Vespasian took control of the campaign, and after he was declared Roman emperor in A.D. 69, his son Titus succeeded him. Once the Romans had broken down resistance in the Jewish countryside, they had only to wait out the siege of Jerusalem. After four years of bloodshed, storming Roman troops entered the sacred Temple, looted its treasures, and burned it to the ground. This total destruction brought to a tragic end a chapter of Jewish history that had begun with the rebuilding of the second temple by Babylonian exiles in 515 B.C.

A few Zealot survivors fled to Herod's rock fortress at Masada, where they held out for nearly three years against another Roman siege. Once their cause was clearly lost, the revolutionaries committed mass suicide rather than submit to Rome.

After the war, land in Palestine was appropriated and entrusted to those who were loyal to Rome. The province was given imperial rank, the tenth legion encamped there, and all Jews were forced to pay Rome the annual half-shekel tax that they were accustomed to contribute annually for the daily sacrifices at the Temple in Jerusalem. A new era of heavier and much more severe oppression had begun, an era that profoundly influenced Judaism and the Christian movement.

Postwar Judaism and Mark's Community

The Sadducees did not survive the catastrophe of A.D. 70 as a significant movement within Judaism. With the Temple destroyed, their power based in Jerusalem disappeared, and the Sadducees did not seem to have the resilience needed to play a significant role in the postwar reconstruction. Their rigid and conservative adherence to the letter of the Law, their resistance to change, and their denial of the resurrection made them ill-equipped to lead the people in restoring their religious pride. Also, during the revolt of A.D. 66-70 the Romans destroyed the monastery at Qumran. The Essene movement died out, apparently unable to find a place in Jewish life.

Unlike the Sadducees and Essenes, the Pharisees played a most significant role in the period of reconstruction. The Temple was gone, but synagogues could be founded and rebuilt. Sacrifices at Jerusalem had ceased, but the Law, that other pillar of Judaism, remained in place. The Pharisees, as interpreters of the Law, survived the ordeal under Rome and retained an untarnished reputation among the people. They assumed almost exclusive power within Judaism by discrediting the Sadducees, their only remaining rivals, and by restraining the power of the traditional priesthood. Pharisees began to regulate the religious calendar, assumed the right to limit the conduct of priests in synagogue worship, transferred a part of the Temple ritual to the synagogue, and established norms governing the collection of gifts and offerings previously due to the Temple. Within Pharisaism conflicts over the Law were gradually resolved in favor of more liberal interpretations, and codification was slowly introduced to systematize the previously chaotic interpretation of the Law. Also in the interests of unification and to capitalize on popular sentiment, the Pharisees attempted to regulate the synagogue worship by making its service resemble that of the destroyed Temple in Jerusalem. They standardized the traditional service, concentrated on establishing the canon of scripture, and instituted the rabbinate as the official body authorized to interpret the Law.

The Pharisaic reconstruction came into direct conflict with the Christian movement. The Pharisees saw the Christians as a potential threat to their power. Therefore, they introduced into Jewish synagogues liturgical practices aimed at eliminating the Christian religious movement that was steadily gaining in significance. The postwar rise of Pharisaism profoundly influenced the Christians, whose roots were buried so deep in Judaism. Christian-Jews questioned their relationship to postwar Judaism. Should they continue as a sect within Judaism? Should they accept or reject the understanding of Judaism promoted by the Pharisees? Were they to continue their mission to the Jews, or should they turn more attention to the gentiles? What about the clouds of tension, hostility, and persecution gathering in the synagogues? How should they understand the controversies between themselves and the synagogue leaders, and what were they to make of their expulsion from the synagogues for making messianic claims about Jesus?

Mark's gospel, written immediately after the Jewish war, informed and influenced Christian communities as they faced these critical questions about their identity. Later, this first gospel would serve as a written source for Matthew, who in A.D. 85 incorporated most of Mark's text into a gospel written for predominantly Christian Jews who were in explicit dialogue with the Pharisaic movement. Still later, as we will see, John wrote his gospel within a tradition different from those of Mark and Matthew, but for diaspora communities already expelled from the synagogues. Nevertheless, each gospel tells the story of Jesus, and each addresses Christians engaged in a struggle for their identity—a struggle to make meaning of their lives in times of deep religious and cultural transition.

Keeping in mind the historical reconstruction of postwar Judaism, and noting the differences in culture and the distance in time, I would like to suggest some resemblances between the period of transition in which Mark wrote his gospel and the setting in which we read it. For we, too, have begun to experience a period of deep transition in our Christian churches as well as in the secular world—the world of economic, political, military, industrial, family, educational, and technological institutions.

What happens in a time of transition? First, events break in upon the community that cause its members to question their current behavior (are we doing the right thing?) and even their own identity (who are we?). Different people respond very differently to the changing situation. Attempts to answer these questions trigger disorientation, confusion, and tension, and often lead to conflict. Some want to hang on to the past, cut out what no longer fits, and put new life into traditional patterns of behavior. Others want to accommodate the past, adjust to the new situation, facilitate gradual growth and development that harmonizes with the past. Still others want to break cleanly with the past, create unique solutions, and introduce a total transformation or revolution.

Such pluralism and confusion drive the community back to its roots to rediscover and reclaim the persons and experiences that gave birth to the community. Then and only then can it meet the present, address its challenges, and move creatively into the future. Exploring the past enables the community to formulate a stronger, more appropriate self-identity, to create new perspectives from which to view its changed situation, and finally to choose more effective patterns of behavior and strategies for action.

Present-day experiences of transition are similar to those of Mark's community. Events in Rome and Judaea—principally the Jewish war and the ensuing destruction of Jerusalem and the Temple—precipitated a crisis and brought change to Mark and his community. The impact of these events made the young Christian community wonder about its place within Judaism, and the questions that emerged caused confusion, tension, and conflict within the community. Mark addressed the identity question by relating it to the life of Jesus, their Messiah. Using earlier traditions, he wrote a narrative, a story about Jesus from his baptism by John at the Jordan to the announcement in Galilee of his resurrection. Through the story, Mark showed his community that following Jesus required a willingness to suffer as he had suffered; dedication to the mission he had given them, and patient waiting in hope for his coming as the triumphant Son of Man. Mark wanted his story to renew his community's sense that they were followers of Jesus and to empower them to live effectively in the chaotic world of postwar Judaism.

Similarly, change today, whether in the Christian churches or in the secular world, means living in a global village where we feel we have lost control over the economy, the arms race, international terrorism; it means helplessly watching the expansion of the drug culture, disruption in marriage and family life, and an alarming increase in violence and crime. These events bombard us through the media and remind us daily that we are experiencing a deep transition in our world and that we are not at all certain of the outcome. We begin to ask questions. What are we to do? Is the world rushing to a foreordained, tragic climax, which we are powerless to prevent? Or can the present world still be redeemed? Can we still come together to effect change toward a better world? Such questions disorient and confuse us, and we respond with very different answers.

In the next chapter we will explore how, by entering into Mark's gospel, we might gain a stronger sense of ourselves as Christians, find out what it means to live as Christians in today's world, and choose to live out of the values portrayed in this gospel.

4

Mark's Story: The Gospel Itself

In reconstructing the world behind Mark's gospel, we made meaningful contact with the historical situation common to the evangelist and his community—their expectations and feelings, their struggle for identity in postwar Judaism. Now we want to look at the gospel itself, at its power to disclose to all readers in every age a way of looking at reality and of making meaning of everyday life.

The historical viewpoint we have just explored must be complemented by approaching the gospel of Mark as a story. We will first discuss the theme of the gospel—Jesus and the Kingdom of God—in order to identify how the narrative discloses an apocalyptic view of transcendent power beyond the world of immediate experience. We will then study the major characters and their development by watching how Jesus interacts with the Jewish authorities, with the crowds, and with his followers. Next, we will trace the dramatic movement, particularly in the second half of the gospel (8:27—16:8), from the prediction of Jesus' death and resurrection to its fulfillment. We will look closely at Mark's portrayal of Jesus' death and resurrection as a passage through death to glory. In this study of Mark's story, we will discover Mark's message of hope for his community and for us.

This study of Mark will enable you to experience the gospel and to see it in relationship to your life. Mark's gospel may also challenge some of your cherished beliefs. Gradually the strange and foreign land of Mark's gospel will become for you a familiar landscape where you will begin to feel at home. If you enter the narrative with an attitude of reverence and openness, if you let it inform and influence your view of the world, your exploration of Mark's world can enrich your prayer with Mark and become a grace-filled event.

An Apocalyptic World View

Narrative elements in Mark come together, inform, and project an apocalyptic world of transcendent power. What do we mean by *apocalyptic*? What are the characteristics of an apocalyptic view? The word *apocalyptic*, from the Greek *apocalypsis*, means "an uncovering." The apocalyptic movement in Judaism and Christianity claimed that God had revealed secrets about the imminent end of the world and had given a message for his people. Those in the apocalyptic movement were children of both despair and of hope—despair about the present course of human history in the world, and hope in the invincible power of God in the world.

A primary tenet of Jewish faith was that God had created the world and that he ruled all within it. But the Jewish people had experienced more catastrophe than prosperity in this world that their God had created. The Babylonians had conquered Israel and had led them off to exile. The Israelites' eventual return to their land occurred only at the pleasure of the Persian rulers. A brief period of independence under the Maccabeans was followed by Roman conquest, the hated rule of Herod the Great, and direct Roman control over Jerusalem and the Temple. Finally, the revolt against Rome ended with the destruction of city and Temple. The Jews saw their intolerable situation as a sign that human history was rushing headlong to a foreordained tragic end. However, the Jews believed that since God still remained ruler of creation, these events must be part of some divine plan. Once the horrors had come to a dramatic climax, a new age would surely dawn.

This series of climactic events would lead to God's final intervention in human history, directly or through intermediary figures. Through these events, the world would be transformed into a perfect world in which God's people would be forever blessed for their fidelity and their enemies would be forever punished. In the meantime, God's people must endure the struggles, prepare for the new age, and watch for the signs of its coming.

In assembling his gospel, Mark expresses this apocalyptic world view. He uses the symbol "Kingdom of God," the distinctive title "Son of Man," and he portrays with urgency the cosmic struggle between the power of evil and God's kingly power in Jesus of Nazareth.

Kingdom of God

The most significant apocalyptic symbol in Mark is the "Kingdom of God." It appears throughout the gospel, but it is especially important in the inauguration of Jesus' ministry (1:14-15), in his teaching in parables (4:1-34), and in his description of the end-time (13:1-37).

Immediately after John baptizes Jesus in the Jordan (1:9-11), he confronts Satan in the wilderness (1:12-13) and comes to Galilee to preach the gospel message: "The time is fulfilled, and the Kingdom of God is at hand: repent, and believe in the gospel" (1:15). Everything we hear Jesus say and watch him do throughout the rest of the gospel, from this beginning to his final fate at the hands of his enemies, unfolds the meaning of this announcement.

The Jesus of Mark's gospel reveals to those around him the "secret of the Kingdom of God" in parables about the sower, the seed growing secretly, and the mustard seed (4:1-34). These parables invite Mark's readers to see and understand that although Jesus' life and death seemed insignificant, it did in fact inaugurate that final, glorious age—the Kingdom of God. The Kingdom of God is like the apparent failure of the sower who sees most of his seed wasted, a failure transformed into success in an incredible and unexpected harvest, a huge gift of grain from the good ground. Or the Kingdom is like the seed the farmer sowed but then ignored, seed that on its own and in unknown ways produced a rich harvest for the farmer to gather into his barn. Or the Kingdom of God is like the tiny mustard seed that without any effort of the farmer provided the largest shrub in the garden. All three stories stress that the results of humble beginnings cannot be predicted.

From the beginning, Jesus' earthly life appeared so insignificant, hidden, and small that it seemed ridiculous to claim that in him God's Kingdom has dawned. He is misunderstood by the Jewish religious authorities and even by his own family, and his ministry seems a failure. But the parables reveal to those who would see and understand that in the end Jesus will be revealed for what he truly is, the one who inaugurates the new age, God's final glorious rule over creation.

In his farewell discourse (13:1-37), Mark's Jesus reveals the new age to his four closest followers by describing how God's Kingdom will once and for all break into the world. He predicts the stress and tribulation that must precede the new age, and he describes the unmistakable signs that human history is doomed. His followers will experience deceivers in their midst, wars and persecutions, the destruction of the Temple, and general cosmic disorder. Then God will act to complete the new age. The faithful followers will see the Son of Man coming in the clouds of heaven with great power and glory to gather to himself those who have endured to the end and have waited patiently for his coming (13:26-27). In the meantime, the disciples must not fear; they must wait and watch.

Mark and his readers understood the Kingdom of God as an apocalyptic symbol, a way of talking about God's final redemption of the world and of his people in the world. The symbol expressed apocalyptic hope, because to use the expression "Kingdom of God" was to speak of God acting as king, to speak of God visiting and redeeming the people—the central theme in the message of Jesus.

"Kingdom of God," as a symbol, was deeply rooted in the Jewish consciousness of themselves as the people of God. For to the Jews, God, who had created the world, was continually active in that world on behalf of the people. They knew themselves as a people who had successfully escaped from Egypt, settled in Canaan, and built a temple to their God on Mount Zion. God had done these things on their behalf, and by using "Kingdom of God" as a symbol in their songs of praise, they celebrated their history as God's people.

Events before and after the Exile might well have shattered the people's faith in God as a king active on their behalf. But prophets arose to interpret the events as consistent with the Kingdom of God. They preached that catastrophes were God's judgment upon the people for their infidelity and that temporary reprieves revealed a God who still acted on their behalf. Above all, the prophets reinterpreted the Kingdom of God to express hope that God would deliver them from their Assyrian and Babylonian captors, as God had once delivered them from Egypt—a hope that was fulfilled when some of the Jews returned to the promised land and rebuilt the Temple. Within Mark's lifetime, Jerusalem and the Temple had again been destroyed, and the "Kingdom of God" had come to represent the hope that God would act finally to establish a new age and fully redeem the people.

Son of Man

The title "Son of Man" also draws Mark's readers into an apocalyptic world. In Jewish traditions the title designates a more-than-human figure. In the Book of Daniel the title describes the central figure who ultimately receives dominion over all the peoples of the earth (Daniel 7:14). Since the "Son of Man" later is interpreted by Daniel as the "saints of the Most High" (7:18), the figure seems to represent the faithful remnant of Israel rather than an individual person. The title also occurs in later Jewish writings. For example, in the apocryphal book of Enoch, "Son of Man" designates a figure who in the last times will overthrow the wicked and uphold the righteous (1 Enoch 46-53). He is also called the "Anointed One" and the "Elect One," titles that clearly designate him as eschatological deliverer of Israel. In 4 Ezra, a similar eschatological avenger is described. Although his title is simply "Man," it may belong to the "Son of Man" tradition.

Although data from Daniel and the apocryphal books of Enoch yield no firm conclusions about the meaning of the title "Son of Man" to the Jews of Jesus' time, Mark nevertheless found that the title most adequately expressed who Jesus of Nazareth was to the community. At the beginning of his gospel, Mark uses the title to designate Jesus as he ministered in Galilee (2:1-10; 2:27-28). Mark also uses the title to refer to Jesus as the one who was betrayed (14:21) and arrested (14:41), who suffered (9:12) and died (10:45), who was raised from the dead (9:9) and was seated at God's right hand in heaven (14:62), and who would come at the end of the age to gather the faithful into God's Kingdom (13:26).

Throughout Mark's gospel, Jesus alone uses the title "Son of Man." As Jesus cures the paralytic, the scribes challenge his power to forgive sins. Jesus responds: "That you may know that the Son of Man has authority on earth to forgive sins, . . . I say to you [the paralytic], rise, take up your pallet and go home" (2:10-11). When Peter confesses that Jesus is the Christ, Jesus responds that "the Son of Man must suffer many things, and be rejected by the elders and the chief priests and the scribes, and be killed, and after three days rise again" (8:31). Jesus clarifies the meaning of the title "Christ" by predicting that he will be the suffering, dying, and rising "Son of Man," a prediction that expresses a shocking understanding of how the long-awaited Messiah will rescue the Jewish people from Roman oppression. Similarly, in the trial scene when the high priest asks Jesus, "Are you the Christ, the Son of the Blessed?" Jesus accepts the titles, but then goes on, "I am; and you will see the Son of Man sitting at the right hand of Power, and coming with the clouds of heaven" (14:62). He boldly predicts that the Jewish officials will come to see in Jesus' death and resurrection his enthronement as the Son of Man, and that within their lifetime they will also see him coming in glory to establish the Kingdom of God. His enemies understand his words, accuse him of blasphemy, and condemn him to death. Against the Jewish apocalyptic background, Jesus clearly identifies himself as the heavenly Son of Man who in his earthly ministry and in his death and resurrection has come to introduce the new age. He will return soon to bring that age to its completion.

When Mark's special use of the title "Son of Man" describes the paradox of Jesus' suffering and death, he creates a tension in his readers. Taken literally, the triumphant title is incompatible with suffering and death. Mark has brought together realities that do not appear to belong together. Here, Mark allows the tension he has created to work in us. The two apparently incompatible realities will gradually disclose a world in which suffering and glory redefine each other. Mark's gospel discloses this world of values and powers as based on the paradox of

Jesus as the suffering Son of Man. This paradox controls Mark's gospel.

Cosmic struggle

More than the other evangelists, Mark portrays the cosmic struggle between the powers of evil and the Kingdom of God. After his baptism, Mark's Jesus is led by the Spirit into the wilderness to confront Satan, the master of evil (1:12-13). This immediate and direct confrontation initiates the conflict that intensifies in Jesus' preaching, teaching, and healing, in his miracles and his debates with the Jewish religious authorities, and in his passion and death.

After he has resisted Satan's temptations, Jesus publicly announces, as we have seen, that the power of God's Kingdom is at hand, and he calls his hearers to repentance and faith. "The time is fulfilled, and the Kingdom of God is at hand; repent, and believe in the gospel" (1:15).

Throughout the first half of Mark's gospel Jesus plunders Satan's goods and destroys his power by healing those who are sick, by driving demons out of the possessed, and by overcoming the hostile powers in nature. The miracle stories usually have the same outcome and follow the same rhythmic pattern— circumstance, miracle, aftermath. For example, in the first miracle story, that of the man with the unclean spirit, Mark describes the circumstances (1:23-24), recounts the open confrontation between Jesus and the unclean spirit (1:25-26), and describes the impression the miracle produced on the onlookers (1:27):

Circumstances: And immediately there was in their synagogue a man with an unclean spirit; and he cried out, "What have you to do with us, Jesus of Nazareth? Have you come to destroy us? I know who you are, the Holy One of God." (1:23-24)

Miracle: But Jesus rebuked him, saying: "Be silent, and come out of him!" And the unclean spirit, convulsing and crying with a loud voice, came out of him. (1:25-26)

Aftermath: And they were all amazed, so that they mentioned among themselves, saying "What is this? With authority he commands even the unclean spirits, and they obey him." (1:27)

The same pattern occurs in several other stories:

Miracle Story	Circumstances	Miracle	Aftermath
Simon's Mother-in-Law	1:30	1:31a	1:31b
The Paralytic	2:3-4	2:5a, 10b-12a	2:12b
The Storm at Sea	4:35b-38	4:39-40	4:41
The Gerasene Demoniac	5:2b-5	5:6-13	5:14-17
Jairus's Daughter	5:22-24, 35-40	5:41-42a	5:42b-43
The Woman Who Touched Jesus' Garment	5:25-28	5:29	5:30-34
The Deaf and Dumb Man	7:32	7:33-35	7:36-37
The Blind Man	8:22	8:23-25	8:26

By describing the circumstances, Mark shows how faith is the disposition needed before Jesus can perform a miracle. Faith means the people recognized their need, were convinced that Jesus had the power to meet it, and expressed that conviction in word and/or action. When Simon and Andrew tell Jesus that Simon's mother-in-law lies sick with a fever, their words carry the conviction that Jesus can heal her. Four men bring a paralytic to Jesus as a gesture of their confidence in his power. During the storm at sea, the disciples awaken Jesus with the cry "Teacher, do you not care if we perish?" Jairus falls at Jesus' feet with the faith-filled request that he make his daughter well. The woman with the hemorrhage reasons to herself that she only needs to touch Jesus' garment to be healed, and she hears Jesus say, "Daughter, your faith has made you well." The deaf and dumb man's friends make the same request. All these words and gestures reveal that those who come to Jesus are convinced that God's kingly power is present and active in him. Where such faith was lacking (for example, in his own country), Jesus' power over evil was severely limited.

The miracles dramatize the confrontation between Jesus and the power of evil in different guises—possession, disease, storms, death. Without apparent effort Jesus wins each confrontation and rescues the persons from the evil that gripped them. His actions reveal God's kingly power at work in the world, and his miracles are visible signs of God's power over evil.

Since the practice of medicine was primitive in Jesus' day, the blind and the lame, the lepers and the possessed were judged victims of an overpowering evil force and were pushed into the background of society. The blind and the lame scattered along the roadside begging for coins from passersby. Lepers, condemned and banned from town and temple, moved in bands across the countryside. Epileptics and psychotics roamed wild among the tombs, or, cruelly manacled, rolled on the ground and shrieked uncontrollable, lunatic noises. Since these persons were perceived as victims of the power of evil, Jesus' miracles revealed victory over that power. They were a sign that the ultimate victory, assured but not yet complete, was at hand; God had begun to rule creation in absolute power. By casting out demons and healing the sick, Jesus also empowered those who had no power, the marginal and the oppressed, to participate in the life and culture of their society. Jesus' miracles, then, revealed the Kingdom of God, showed his compassion for the powerless and possessed, and empowered the marginal and oppressed.

Jesus' confrontations with the Jewish religious authorities also represent the power of evil struggling against God's power in Jesus. When confronted by these authorities, especially the scribes and Pharisees, Mark's Jesus overcomes their challenge and reduces them to silence. For example, toward the beginning of his Galilean ministry, opponents question Jesus about his activities, but he wins each debate and remains victorious over their evil intentions (2:1-3:6). Each confrontation is couched in a short story that culminates in a saying of Jesus. The saying may be evoked by a friendly or by a hostile question, or the saying may be associated with an incident described in few words. Characteristically, though, the story interest remains secondary to Jesus' saying or to his dialogue with the religious authorities. (Incidentally, Mark's community prized these sayings because they provided guidance in everyday life—Jesus had spoken, and nothing more need be said; they must now live according to his words.)

Five conflict stories occur early in Mark's gospel. Each story follows a definite pattern: setting, test question, response. For example, in the first conflict story, Jesus is in the midst of curing the paralytic when the scribes question his power to forgive sins. Mark describes the setting (2:3-5), introduces the test question, "Who can forgive sins but God alone?" (2:6-7) and an unmistakeable response follows (2:8-11). The next three episodes reproduce the same pattern:

Conflict Story	Setting	Test Question	Response
Eating with Sinners	2:16a	2:16b	2:17
Fasting	2:18a	2:18b	2:19-22
Plucking Grain	2:23	2:24	2:25-28

In the final conflict story about the man with a withered hand, the pattern is altered. Mark describes the setting (3:1-3), then alters the questioning—Jesus asks the test question, but the Pharisees do not respond (3:4). Jesus then cures the man (3:5), and the Pharisees "hold counsel with the Herodians against him how to destroy him" (3:6). This scene with its broken pattern brings the sequence to a dramatic climax. Our interest is focused not so much on the cure as on the tension that has been building between Jesus and the Pharisees over the Sabbath observance, a tension that leads the authorities to determine to put Jesus to death. For what seems on the surface to be ordinary skirmishes between the Jewish religious authorities and a Jew from Nazareth are in fact struggles between evil powers at work in the established religious authorities and God's power, the Kingdom of God, at work in Jesus of Nazareth.

We have studied the symbol "Kingdom of God," the title "Son of Man," and the confrontations between Jesus and evil— in the desert, in his miracles, and in his debates with the Jewish authorities. These elements combine to disclose the apocalyptic world to Mark's community. The members of that community confronted evil in postwar Judaism, and they vacillated between hope and despair. Jesus seemed absent when they needed him most, but they hoped that he would come soon to gather them into the Kingdom.

What will happen when we interact with Mark's apocalyptic world? It is difficult to predict, since that world is so different and distant from the one in which we live. We do not live in an apocalyptic age. Or do we? Some may find themselves unable to participate in such a totally strange and foreign landscape. Others may find themselves at home with elements like the miracle stories but not with the total world view. Still others may take Mark's story seriously without taking it literally. In prayer they choose to enter that story and participate in it. In the preceding chapter, for example, we saw how Lucy, Marie, and Steve let Mark's story become their story, and their story become Mark's story. They let Mark's world inform and influence how they make meaning in their search for God.

Characters and Their Development

In our introduction to Mark we saw that the evangelist created character, and I suggested that watching the characters interact might be a fruitful focus in reading the entire gospel. Now that you are familiar with the text, I want to take a closer look at the relationships among the characters. Let me recall the scheme we used to illustrate those relationships.

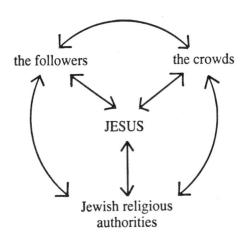

The category "Jewish religious authorities" includes those from the various interest groups who are openly hostile to Jesus and his followers. They consist of the Pharisees, the scribes, the Herodians, the Sadducees, the chief priests, the elders, and the high priest. Throughout the gospel they challenge Jesus' words and actions; they raise questions to test him about forgiving sin (2:7), eating with sinners and tax collectors (2:16), plucking grain on the Sabbath (2:24), being possessed by Beelzebul (3:22), eating with unwashed hands (7:5), giving a sign from heaven (8:11), allowing divorce (10:2), exercising his authority (11:27), paying tribute to Caesar (12:14), believing in the resurrection (12:18), and valuing the great commandment (12:28). As we have seen in these debates, Jesus stands against the Jewish religious authorities, arguing without compromise and winning every encounter. At times he responds to their hostility with strong language (7:6,9; 12:9,38). He is fully confident of his own positions, and he sees little truth in their positions. We have seen that Mark records these skirmishes to reveal the underlying struggle between evil power at work in the Jewish authorities and God's power at work in Jesus. God clearly wins the struggle with evil.

Throughout the narrative the Jewish religious authorities also plot to put Jesus to death. After their initial debates, the Pharisees "went out, and immediately held counsel with the Herodians against him, how to destroy him" (3:6). Almost from the beginning, an ominous shadow is cast over the story, and we are invited to ask, "Will the Pharisees actually carry out their plan?" Foreshadowings occur more frequently as Jesus draws near his suffering and death (11:18; 12:12; 14:1-2; 14:10-11). The chief priests and the scribes plot to arrest him (14:1-2), and they arrange with Judas to have him betrayed (14:10-11). Jewish religious authorities later gather in solemn council to put Jesus on trial. The climax comes when the high priest confronts Jesus:

> Again the high priest asked him, "Are you the Christ, the Son of the Blessed?" And Jesus said, "I am; and you will see the Son of Man sitting at the right hand of Power, and coming with the clouds of heaven." And the high priest tore his mantle, and said, "Why do we still need witnesses? You have heard his blasphemy. What is your decision?" And they all condemned him as deserving death. (14:61b-64)

The next morning, the council takes Jesus to Pilate (15:1), and during the trial they stir the crowd to have Barabbas released and Jesus crucified (15:6-15). In their final appearance in the narrative, they taunt Jesus as he hangs on the cross: "He saved others; he cannot save himself. Let the Christ, the King of Israel, come down now from the cross, that we may see and believe" (15:31b-32). It appears that in the end Jesus has lost the struggle with the Jewish religious authorities. But their victory is momentary and illusory, since Jesus is vindicated by his resurrection (16:1-8), sits at the right hand of Power (14:62), and will return as the triumphant Son of Man (13:24-27).

In contrast to the Jewish religious authorities, the "crowds" at first respond to Jesus' words and actions with wonder, amazement, and enthusiasm. In Galilee they come to be healed and to hear him preach and teach.

> And many were gathered together, so that there was no longer room for them, not even about the door; and he was preaching the word to them.

> And they came, bringing to him a paralytic carried by four men. (2:2-3)

Jesus withdrew with his disciples to the sea, and a great multitude from Galilee followed; also from Judea and Jerusalem and Idumea and from beyond the Jordan and from about Tyre and Sidon a great multitude, hearing all that he did, came to him. (3:7-8)

Then he went home and the crowd came together again, so that they could not even eat. (3:19-20)

Again he began to teach beside the sea. And a very large crowd gathered about him, so that he got into a boat and sat in it on the sea; and the whole crowd was beside the sea on the land. (4:1)

And when Jesus had crossed again in the boat to the other side, a great crowd gathered about him; and he was beside the sea. (5:21)

These summary statements make it clear that in the early part of the gospel Jesus is portrayed as having attracted large crowds to hear his teaching and to be healed. Astonished at Jesus' words and actions, they are even more amazed as the story progresses.

And they were all amazed, so that they questioned among themselves, saying, "What is this? A new teaching? With authority he commands even the unclean spirits, and they obey him." (1:27)

And he rose, and immediately took up the pallet and went out before them all; so that they were all amazed and glorified God, saying, "We never saw anything like this!" (2:12)

And they were astonished beyond measure, saying, "He has done all things well; he even makes the deaf hear and the dumb speak." (7:37)

Within the crowds, individuals—such as the woman who touched Jesus' garment and Jairus, who asked Jesus to make his daughter well—expressed their faith in Jesus. These individuals become models of faith for us; in approaching Jesus, they recognize their need, are convinced that Jesus has power to meet that need, and express their conviction in word and/or action. Their faith enables them to seek out Jesus and to ask him to heal them, but we are not told that after the cure they left everything to become his followers. The text discloses only that they returned to their previous lives, grateful for the cure and amazed at the power at work in Jesus of Nazareth.

Though enthusiastic about his preaching, teaching, and healing, the crowds as such do not become disciples. They have enough faith in him to seek out his teaching and to bring their sick to be healed, but they fail to make the more radical commitment to leave everything and follow him.

As Jesus enters Jerusalem, the crowds that go before him and those that follow cry out: "Hosanna! Blessed is he who comes in the name of the Lord! Blessed is the kingdom of our father David that is coming! Hosanna in the highest!" (11:9-10). The crowds gladly listen to him teaching in the temple (12:37), but at his trial they let themselves be influenced by the Jewish authorities and ask Pilate to release Barabbas and have Jesus crucified (15:11). Amazement and wonderment at Jesus' words and actions are not strong enough. The crowds yield to pressure from Jesus' enemies, who are intent on putting him to death.

Discipleship in Mark means "following Jesus," that is, literally walking behind him as he ministers in Galilee and journeys to Jerusalem. But following Jesus also means patterning one's life after his by sharing his work and by making Jesus' world view—its symbols and myths, its images of power and centers of value—one's own. The followers can be visualized according to their closeness to Jesus.

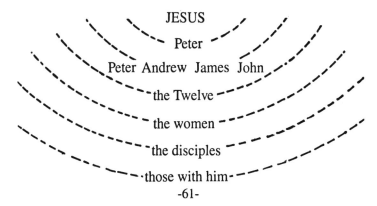

Now we want to look in greater detail at how Mark's Jesus relates to these followers. As we will see, not all followers respond to Jesus with the same generosity, and even those closest to him vacillate between enthusiasm and fear, faith and doubt, understanding and misunderstanding, loyalty and cowardice.

In three stories Mark tells how Jesus called Simon and Andrew, James and John (1:16-20) and Levi (2:13-14) to follow him. The three stories follow the same pattern:

Story	Setting	Call	Reaction
Simon and Andrew	1:16	1:17	1:18
James and John	1:19	1:20a	1:20b
Levi	2:13	2:14a	2:14b

The pattern established in the first two passages (1:16-18 and 1:19-20) is echoed in the scene with Levi (2:13-14).

In the first scene Jesus calls Simon and Andrew: "Follow me and I will make you fishers of men" (1:17), and they leave their nets to share in Jesus' work for the Kingdom. In the call of James and John, Mark emphasizes their response: "They left their father Zebedee in the boat with the hired servants, and followed him" (1:20). Both Jesus' call and the men's response carry a tone of urgency.

The same pattern is repeated in the call of a tax collector named Levi (2:14). He is despised for practicing extortion against his fellow Jews and for collaborating with the hated Romans. But Jesus sees him and says, "Follow me." Levi gets up from his money-table and follows him. Jesus' call to this marginal tax collector is totally gratuitous; as with the fishermen, Levi's response is immediate and radical. In all three stories, Jesus meets these men in their everyday world and calls them to begin a new life as his followers. His call carries within it the demand for a permanent leave-taking from both family and occupation.

This demand, which seems so harsh, concretizes Jesus' urgent proclamation: "The time is fulfilled, and the Kingdom of God is at hand; repent, and believe in the gospel" (1:15). With this announcement Jesus marks the beginning of the long-awaited age in which God will redeem his people and establish forever his Kingdom over all the earth. People must repent—that is, turn their lives upside down to meet the demands of the new age. After recording Jesus' urgent announcement, Mark tells the three call stories which show concretely that repentance can entail a radical discontinuity with one's previous life. Mark and his community, who were experiencing strong discontinuity with postwar Judaism, would surely have interpreted these stories in light of that experience. Jesus' call to follow him remained no less urgent and radical.

From the large group of followers, Mark's Jesus chooses twelve "to be with him, and to be sent out to preach and have authority to cast out demons" (3:14). Jesus invites the Twelve to participate more deeply in his life and work through sharing friendship and common life ("being with him") and through collaborating in his work ("to be sent out"). He affirms companionship and ministry, community and mission, being and doing as complementary values.

Later Jesus models both values. He sends the Twelve out, two by two, and gives them authority over unclean spirits (6:7). Jesus entrusts his own work to the Twelve, and they begin to participate in and exercise his power. They preach and heal, as they have seen their master preach and heal. By sharing this power with them, Jesus shows trust and confidence in the Twelve. Mark summarizes the results: "So they went out and preached that men should repent. And they cast out many demons and anointed with oil many that were sick and healed them" (6:12-13). Their success indicates that Jesus' trust was well placed. Finally, when the Twelve return to report their success, Jesus invites them, "Come away by yourselves to a lonely place, and rest awhile" (6:31). They go away together in a boat to a place by themselves, but their plans to be together simply for rest and companionship are thwarted when crowds come from the surrounding towns to hear Jesus' teaching. Nevertheless, the story reveals the importance of balancing the values of ministry to others with the ministry of companionship among themselves.

In episodes concerning bread Jesus reveals how, as Messiah, he leads people through the desert and enables them truly to see and to hear the meaning of his words and actions (6:33-8:26). His followers either misunderstand altogether or at best show only a partial understanding of his words and actions. They are terrified when Jesus walks toward them on the water, and they are astonished when he gets into the boat and calms the storm (6:49-50, 52). They lack understanding when they ask Jesus to explain his parable (7:17), and they fail to see what the surplus of bread at the two multiplications meant (6:34-44 and 8:1-9). Jesus' followers understand something of their master's words and deeds, but they misunderstand their deeper meaning.

The cure of the blind man (8:22-26) is an allegory that symbolizes how Jesus' followers will grow only gradually in their understanding of his life and ministry. The blind man is cured in two stages. First, Jesus puts spittle on the man's eyes and lays his hand on him. The blind man begins to see men, but they appear to him like trees walking. Only after Jesus imposes hands a second time does the man see everything clearly.

This story functions as a preface to the scene at Caesarea Philippi (8:27-30), where it becomes clear that the disciples have come from blindness to partial sight about Jesus as the Messiah. In this key episode, Peter, speaking for the others, professes that Jesus is the Christ, the Messiah. Peter's profession marks, as we saw earlier, an important turning point in the gospel's movement. The disciples have seen in Jesus' words and actions that he is the Messiah, that ideal leader sent by God to establish a new age and save the people from Roman domination. The disciples have discovered this "messianic secret." Now they are to confront the "messianic mystery": that precisely as Messiah Jesus must suffer, die, and rise again.

As they begin the journey to Jerusalem, Jesus begins to unfold this "messianic mystery," but his followers fail to understand (8:31-10:45). Jesus instructs them that following him means that they must be ready to walk to Jerusalem, to the suffering and death that await him there, and through that suffering and death to the time when he will come in the glory of the resurrection and second coming. But the disciples misunderstand. They have participated in his work and have shared his power to preach and heal, but they are not ready to accept the mystery of his suffering, death, and resurrection. Mark's portrayal of these disciples suggests that "following Jesus" can involve ambiguity, confusion, and misunderstanding.

At Caesarea Philippi Peter, the follower par excellence, represents the followers in their loyalties and in their failures. Throughout Mark's gospel, we see Peter's leadership role: He is the first one called to follow Jesus (1:16), the first to be given a new name by Jesus (3:16), and in the inner circle of followers is always named first (5:37, 9:2, 13:3, 14:33). He more than anyone speaks for the group (1:36, 8:29, 9:5-6, 10:28, 11:21). At Caesarea Philippi, in a pivotal scene, Peter professes that Jesus is the Christ (8:29), but he immediately misunderstands Jesus' predictions about his suffering, death, and resurrection (8:32b-33). At the transfiguration (9:5-6) Peter, caught between enthusiasm and fear, is at a loss for words. On the way to Gethsemane, Peter declares his loyalty to Jesus (14:29-31), and he watches with Jesus in the garden (14:32-42). But he ends up denying Jesus before the Jews, just as Jesus had predicted (14:66-71), and in Mark's last report of Peter, we read that he broke down and wept in sorrow and repentance for having betrayed his master (14:72).

The women, though more faithful than Peter and the Twelve, portray a similar confusion—especially in Mark's account of their visit to the tomb. Throughout Mark's gospel, women respond positively to Jesus: Simon's mother-in-law (1:31), the woman with the hemorrhage (5:28), the Syrophoenician woman (7:25), and the woman at Bethany who anointed Jesus' body for burial (14:3). The women who followed Jesus and ministered to him in Galilee make the journey with him to Jerusalem. They witness his death (15:40-41) and see where he was buried (15:47).

When they bring spices to anoint his body, they find the tomb empty and hear a young man announce: "He is risen. . . .But go, tell his disciples and Peter that he is going before you to Galilee; there you will see him as he told you" (16:6-7). The women, in fear and trembling, say nothing to anyone, neither to Peter nor to the disciples. Mark's gospel ends without his followers ever hearing the announcement that Jesus is risen.

How did Mark's community see their situation mirrored in the evangelist's portrayal of the Jewish authorities, the crowds, and the followers? Mark's community recognized in the Jewish authorities' constant hostility toward Jesus their own struggles with the Pharisaic movement. The crowds' enthusiasm for Jesus' teaching and their amazement at his healings were not enough to carry them through the experience of suffering. So Mark's community could most strongly identify with those followers. As we have seen, his community struggled also with questions about their identity, especially about their relationship to postwar Judaism. These struggles led to tension, to confusion, and to conflict within the community. Like Jesus' followers in the gospel, they might well have vacillated between commitment to their call and hesitation about its demands. Following Jesus meant risking separation from the synagogues and from their social world. They understood and experienced the "secrets of the Kingdom" in their own situation, but they found it much more difficult to accept the paradox of suffering and to see it at work in their experience. Since they, too, felt overwhelmed with suffering, they might well have felt compassion for the disciples who failed to support Jesus in his hour of trial.

Mark portrayed the characters in his narrative in such a way that members of his community could participate in the story, find themselves in it, and be strengthened in their search for meaning in their lives. Can we also find ourselves in Mark's characters and their development? It seems we can, since, like the followers, we sometimes waver in our commitment to Jesus. We too move between enthusiasm for our Christian call and hesitation about its demands in a secular world. We may participate in the power of the Kingdom, but we also know that its demands bring ridicule and opposition. Sometimes we are filled with faith, but we also grow afraid in the face of violent crimes, inflation, unemployment, hunger, and oppression. We seem to misunderstand more than we understand, and we often find it difficult to live according to the paradox of suffering.

In short, the experience of the followers in Mark's gospel bears a strong resemblance to our own experience. For to follow Jesus in any age means to experience the pull between enthusiasm and fear, faith and doubt, understanding and misunderstanding, suffering and hope. In Christian life, these tensions are inevitable for Jesus' followers as they struggled in the gospel, for Mark and his community as they struggled in their situation, and for us as we struggle to witness to the Kingdom in our time.

Through Suffering to Glory — Mark's Message of Hope

The most coherent and dramatic movement in Mark comes when Jesus journeys with his followers from Galilee to Jerusalem (8:27-10:52), ministers in the Temple (11:1-13:37), and experience his passion, death, and resurrection (14:1-16:8). As we noted in Chapter 1, Mark gives precise indications of geographical movement and the passage of time. Now we want to focus on the dramatic paradox that, as the Son of Man, Jesus must suffer, die, and rise. Jesus predicts that he must pass through suffering to glory. His followers consistently fail to understand. But Jesus' predictions are fulfilled in the story about his passion and death, and in the announcement of his resurrection.

Journey from Galilee to Jerusalem (8:27-10:52)

As we have seen, Peter speaks for himself and the other disciples in the pivotal episode at Caesarea Philippi when he says of Jesus, "You are the Christ" (8:29). Jesus then predicts that, as Son of Man, he must suffer, die and rise again (8:31-32a). With that prediction he announces the theme that dominates the journey from Galilee to Jerusalem. Three times he says he must pass through suffering to glory. Each time his followers fail to understand. And each time Jesus counters their misunderstanding with instructions on what it means to be a disciple.

Prediction	Misunderstanding	Instruction
8:31-32a	8:32b-33	8:34—9:1
9:30-31	9:32	9:33-50
10:32-34	10:35-40	10:41-45

The repeated interplay between Jesus' predictions, the followers' misunderstanding, and his instructions creates tension and suspense in the story. Will Jesus' predictions come true? Will his followers ever understand? Such questions draw us into the drama as we journey with Jesus to Jerusalem.

In each prediction, the title Son of Man is placed over against Jesus' suffering, death, and resurrection. Since it is unthinkable that such a heavenly figure could suffer and die, Jesus' statements seem literally absurd. Only if his followers allow the contradictory terms to act upon each other will they come to see the deeper paradox. But instead of entering into this paradox and letting the contradiction in it disclose a new world, instead of letting a new vision of reality emerge out of the tension between the Son of Man and the prediction of his suffering and death, the disciples remain without understanding.

As Jesus journeys to Jerusalem, his *predictions* become more precise and more detailed. First, he simply announces that his suffering, death, and resurrection are necessary in God's plan for the salvation of the world (8:31-32a). Next, Jesus predicts his betrayal by Judas and his arrest in the garden (9:31). And finally Jesus describes in detail the events of his passion and death: "Behold, we are going up to Jerusalem; and the Son of Man will be delivered to the chief priests and the scribes, and they will condemn him to death, and deliver him to the Gentiles; and they will mock him, and spit upon him, and scourge him, and kill him; and after three days he will rise" (10:33-34). Tension mounts as we wonder whether or not these increasingly precise predictions will in fact be fulfilled.

The disciples' *misunderstanding* also seems to grow as they approach Jerusalem. Peter's rebuke draws a counter-rebuke from Jesus: "Get behind me, Satan! For you are not on the side of God, but of men" (8:32b-33). Mark describes how the disciples reacted to the second prediction—". . . they did not understand the saying, and they were afraid to ask him" (9:32). The disciples then go on to discuss with one another who is the greatest (9:33-34). How thoroughly they misunderstand the second prediction! James and John show the same lack of understanding after the third and most precise prediction. They ask, "Grant us to sit, one at your right hand and one at your left, in your glory" (10:37). We wonder at this point whether the disciples will ever grasp the meaning of what Jesus has predicted about his suffering and death.

Jesus' *instructions,* the third element in the pattern, disclose that following him to Jerusalem means viewing reality as ultimately paradoxical, mysterious, ambiguous, upside down, expecting the reversal of ordinary perspectives—power in weakness, life in death, hope in suffering, greatness in service. In a word, followers of Jesus can expect to experience in their own lives the paradox soon to be revealed in Jesus' passion, death, and resurrection. Several sayings articulate how the disciples are to reproduce that paradox:

> If any man would come after me, let him deny himself and take up his cross and follow me.

> For whoever would save his life will lose it; and whoever loses his life for my sake and the gospels will save it. (8:34-35)

> If any one would be first, he must be last of all and servant of all. (9:35)

> You know that those who are supposed to rule over the Gentiles lord it over them, and their great men exercise authority over them. But it shall not be so among you; but whoever would be great among you must be your servant, and whoever would be first among you must be slave of all. For the Son of Man also came not to be served, but to serve, and to give his life as a ransom for many. (10:42-45)

Paradoxical behavior—losing one's life to save it, being great by being servant, being first by being slave of all—marks as disciples those who reproduce in their own lives the pattern of Jesus' suffering, death, and resurrection. For as Jesus came to serve others and to give his life as a ransom, so those who follow him to Jerusalem are to serve others even to death.

Jesus predicts two other events. First, he links the disciples' behavior to the end-time, ". . . when he comes in the glory of his Father with the holy angels" (8:38). Secondly, he connects the coming of the Son of Man with the imminent coming of the Kingdom of God: "There are some standing here who will not taste death before they see the kingdom of God come with power" (9:1). We wonder how Jesus' predictions about the end-time will be fulfilled.

The transfiguration also contributes suspense to the narrative (9:2-8). Peter, James, and John go off with Jesus and witness his transfiguration. They see Elijah and Moses appear and converse with Jesus, and they hear a heavenly voice tell them that Jesus is God's beloved Son. The disciples seem not to understand what they witness, and Jesus charges them to tell no one what they have seen, until the Son of Man has risen from the dead. The disciples carry out the charge, but they also ponder what rising from the dead might mean (9:9-10). Reference to the resurrection suggests that the disciples will one day understand what they do not yet understand: the meaning of Jesus' passion and death. In the transfiguration, they experience a post-resurrection moment, but for now they continue to misunderstand its meaning.

To summarize. The journey to Jerusalem (8:27-10:52) draws us into the movement of Mark's story and focuses our attention on what is to come. Jesus' *predictions*—about the Son of Man's death and resurrection, about his coming in the glory of his Father, and about the imminent arrival of the Kingdom of God—focus attention on the future and sharpen interest in whether or not those predictions will be fulfilled. The followers' *misunderstanding* of Jesus' predictions makes us ask whether they will ever come to see what the predictions mean. Jesus' *instructions* teach that following him means to accept the paradox of his death and resurrection as the value on which to base their actions. It remains to see how the drama in these episodes will be resolved in what takes place in Jerusalem.

Ministry in the Temple (11:1-13:37)

When Jesus and his followers enter Jerusalem and cleanse the Temple, they inaugurate a time of direct confrontation with the Jewish religious authorities, a confrontation between the Kingdom of God and the powers of evil. These episodes (11:27—12:34) provide an *interlude* between the predictions uttered on the journey to Jerusalem and their fulfillment in Jesus' death and resurrection. Through a series of confrontations, the hostility between Jesus and the Jewish religious authorities, already tense in Galilee, grows toward a resolution to have Jesus put to death.

In four pronouncement stories, the Jews test Jesus about his authority, about paying tribute to Caesar, about the resurrection, and about the great commandment. Each story follows the same pattern:

Story	Setting	Test Question	Response
Authority	11:27	11:28	11:29-33
Tribute to Caesar	12:13	12:14-15a	12:15b-17
Resurrection	12:18	12:19-23	12:24-27
Great Commandment	12:28a	12:28b	12:29-34

In each story Jewish religious authorities confront Jesus with a test question, and he responds with a counter-question or a statement that leads to a dialogue. The hostility in the first three scenes is softened in the fourth when an honest, inquiring scribe hears Jesus say, "You are not far from the Kingdom of God" (12:34).

After these confrontations the Jews question Jesus no further, but Jesus questions *them* about the Messiah, "How can the scribes say that the Christ is the Son of David?" (12:35). The Jewish authorities make no response; the crowds, however, hear Jesus' words with gladness (12:35-37). These clear victories over those who are plotting his death reveal again that in Jesus the power of God's Kingdom triumphs over the evil power behind his enemies.

After leaving the Temple area, Jesus presents a clear vision of the future to Peter and Andrew, James and John—the disciples whom he had first invited to follow him (1:16-20). He tells them that they can expect to suffer wars, persecutions, and all manner of hardship, but that in the end God will overthrow the present age and establish the longed-for Kingdom. Jesus' long discourse (comparable only to the parable discourse of 4:1-34) falls into three parts: signs preceding the inbreaking of the Kingdom (13:5-23); the coming of the Son of Man (13:24-27); and exhortations to be watchful (13:28-37). Events predicted in this discourse lie beyond the time encompassed by the gospel story and extend to the second coming of the Son of Man.

In predictions, instructions, and warnings, Jesus says that a time of intense suffering and tribulation will signal the final approach of the Kingdom. In 13:5-23, Mark describes these events in a pattern:

A 5-6 Deceivers

   B 7-8 Wars

      C 9-13 Persecution

   B 14-20 War and Destruction of the Temple

A 21-23 Deceivers

Deceivers, false Christs, and false prophets will show signs and wonders to lead the elect astray (13:6,22). Wars and rumors of wars may cause some to think the end has come, but the end is not yet (13:7). People will first see nation rise against nation and kingdom against kingdom; they will experience earthquakes, famines, and even a desolating sacrilege in the Temple (13:8,14). Worst of all, however, Jesus' followers will be persecuted not only by Jewish religious authorities and by pagan governors and kings (13:9) but also by members of their own families (13:12). Indeed, "you will be hated by all for my name's sake" (13:13). But in such tribulation as has not been seen from the beginning of the creation and will never be seen again (13:19), the disciples are to preach the gospel to all nations (13:10). As Jesus did, they are to carry out their mission in the face of hostility and oppression.

Jesus then describes a vision of the final collapse of the cosmos, the coming of the Son of Man, the inbreaking of the Kingdom, and the gathering of the elect.

> But in those days, after that tribulation, the sun will be darkened, and the moon will not give its light, and the stars will be falling from heaven, and the powers in the heavens will be shaken. And then they will see the Son of Man coming in clouds with great power and glory. And then he will send out the angels, and gather his elect from the four winds, from the ends of the earth to the ends of heaven. (13:24-27)

This vision of the future gives the disciples a reason to hope, even as they anticipate intense tribulation. If they wait with patience and watch, he will return to give them a share in his glory, the glory of God's Kingdom. However, Jesus will not be with them in their struggles. Though risen and seated at the right hand of God, he will remain more absent than present. His disciples will carry out their mission and experience suffering and persecution without a sense of his presence. The disciples draw hope from Jesus' vision of a triumphant future, a total reversal of their present tribulations. We wonder how these extraordinary events will come to pass.

Passion-resurrection narrative (14:1 — 16:8)

Scenes in the introduction to the passion-resurrection narrative (14:1-42) continue the suspense created and sustained throughout the journey from Galilee to Jerusalem (8:27-10:52). The Jewish religious authorities make final plans to put Jesus to death, but for fear of causing a tumult they hesitate to arrest him during the Feast of Unleavened Bread (14:1-2). When Judas Iscariot offers to betray his master (14:10-11), the final confrontation between Jesus and the Jewish authorities is at hand.

As Jesus comes closer to his passion and death, he predicts other events. For example, by anointing Jesus' feet, the woman at Bethany prepares his body for burial (14:8-9). At the Passover meal Jesus predicts that one of the Twelve will betray him

(14:18-21). On the way to the Mount of Olives, Jesus further predicts that at his arrest the Twelve will be scattered, and that Peter will deny him. But he also promises that after his resurrection he will go before them into Galilee (14:26-31). In other words, the Twelve, who have misunderstood Jesus' predictions about his death and resurrection, will act out their misunderstanding in betrayal, flight, and denial. Will they ever understand? Perhaps, when they meet the risen Jesus in Galilee. We must wait and watch the action unfold.

Jesus' prayer in the garden

In his prayer in the garden, Jesus confronts his fate and begins to know a sorrow that threatens his life (14:32-42). He prays with deep distress: "Abba, Father, all things are possible to thee: remove this cup from me; yet not what I will, but what thou wilt" (14:36). As an obedient son, Jesus places himself fully in his Father's hands, and he teaches his closest followers—Peter, James, and John—that they must watch and pray with him in his time of trial and temptation. Through his prayer, Jesus recognizes that he must pass through his passion and death to the glory of his resurrection and his return as the triumphant Son of Man. With resolute steps he walks out of the garden to meet Judas his betrayer and the arresting party: "Rise, let us be going; see my betrayer is at hand" (14:42).

Jesus' arrest

Judas comes accompanied by an armed rabble dispatched by the Jewish religious authorities to arrest him in the garden (14:43-52). According to Jewish custom, disciples greeted their rabbi with a kiss to express loyalty and devotion. When Judas kisses Jesus, he uses that sign to betray his master and signal his arrest. In his betrayal he fulfills what Jesus has predicted (9:32; 14:10-11; 14:17-21). At this point, the disciples flee, also as Jesus predicted: "You will all fall away" (14:27). As Jesus is seized, a young man is also seized. He leaves behind the linen cloth that has been his only clothing and runs away naked. After his death Jesus will be wrapped in a linen cloth for burial, and a young man will appear at the empty tomb to announce the resurrection. Scholars conjecture that this anonymous "young man" may symbolize those who proclaim the news of Jesus' death and resurrection.

Jewish trial

Jesus' public testimony at the Jewish trial is framed by Peter's denial (14:53-72) as if to indicate that while Jesus remains faithful to his Father's will until death, Peter proves unfaithful to his master. Needing evidence against Jesus, his enemies surround him with false witnesses. But the witnesses fail to agree among themselves about Jesus' claim to destroy the Temple and in three days build another. At the moment of his death this claim will be remembered when the Temple veil will be torn from top to bottom. Later the Romans will destroy Jerusalem and the Temple in the Jewish war (A.D. 66-70). After that war Mark's community will look to Jesus as a replacement of the Temple. They may well have seen their experience foreshadowed in Jesus' trial before the Sanhedrin.

When pressed by the high priest to respond to the charges against him, Jesus remains silent. So the high priest is forced to take direct action, and his dialogue with Jesus marks an important dramatic moment. In the first verse of the gospel, Jesus was identified as Christ (Messiah) and Son of God (1:1), and at Caesarea Philippi, Peter professed him to be the Christ (8:29). Now the Jewish high priest uses the same titles as a challenge, and Jesus publicly discloses for the first time the secret that he is the Messiah. He acknowledges before the Jewish Sanhedrin that he is indeed the Christ and Son of God. He then goes on to interpret these titles with reference to the Son of Man: " . . . you will see the Son of Man sitting at the right hand of Power, and coming with the clouds of heaven" (14:62).

With this public confession Jesus incriminates himself before his Jewish accusers, and his claim provokes the death sentence. The charge of blasphemy is not lodged against Jesus because he claimed to be the Christ and Son of God, but because he claimed to be the triumphant Son of Man. The high priest tears his mantle as a formal judicial gesture of condemnation, and members of the Sanhedrin strike him and mock him as a prophet. Jesus' final, direct confrontation with the Jewish religious authorities ends with their sentence of death. These actions fulfill what Jesus predicted in detail as he was nearing Jerusalem: ". . . the Son of Man will be delivered to the chief priests and the scribes, and they will condemn him to death" (10:33).

Peter's denial

Below in the courtyard Peter faces his darkest hour (14:66-72). At first he tries to evade the maid's remark by denying that he understands what she means. As she persists, Peter denies that he is a follower of Jesus. Finally, calling down God's wrath upon himself, he says "I do not know this man of whom you speak" (14:71). Peter dissociates himself completely from Jesus, but a cockcrow jars him into remembering how Jesus had predicted his denial (14:30-31). Shattered, Peter breaks down and weeps. Peter may not understand Jesus' passion and death, but he does repent of his denial.

Trial before Pilate

After a brief consultation the next morning, the Jewish Sanhedrin delivers Jesus to Pilate for trial and execution (15:1-20). Pilate asks Jesus whether he is the political king whom the Jews expected to overthrow the Romans. Jesus acknowledges Pilate's designation: "You have said so" (15:2). The Jewish chief priests then press charges against him, but Jesus keeps the silence appropriate to a suffering just man.

The Jewish crowd asks Pilate to honor the custom of releasing a prisoner at Passover time. Pilate asks them to choose between Jesus, their king, and Barabbas, a man who committed murder in an insurrection. The Jewish chief priests immediately act: "But the chief priests stirred up the crowd to have him release Barabbas instead" (15:11). These religious authorities are clearly more responsible for Jesus' death than are the Jewish crowds. The evil power at work in them seems to win the final victory over God's kingly power in Jesus. Pilate, though convinced of Jesus' innocence, yields to pressure. He heeds their cry for Jesus' death, releases Barabbas the murderer, and condemns the innocent Jesus to be crucified.

To highlight Jesus as king of the Jews, Roman soldiers lead him inside Pilate's palace, clothe him in a purple cloak, and put a crown of thorns on his head. They salute him: "Hail, King of the Jews!" (15:18). They then strike his head with a reed, spit upon him, and kneel to do him homage. Their actions fulfill Jesus' prediction: "and they will mock him, and spit upon him, and scourge him, and kill him" (10:34). They also show that Jesus is king, *not* according to the Roman understanding of political power, but according to the paradox being revealed in his suffering and death.

Crucifixion and death

Mark's gospel reaches its climax in Jesus' struggle and death on the cross. It was customary for the condemned criminal to carry his own cross beam, but a certain Simon of Cyrene is forced to take up the cross for Jesus. Jesus refuses the drugged wine traditionally provided condemned criminals to lessen their pain. The soldiers crucify him and then, as was their custom, roll dice for his clothes. The title on the cross announces Jesus' enthronement as King of the Jews.

As Jesus hangs on the cross, two sets of taunts are hurled at him. Passersby wag their heads, deride Jesus for claiming power to destroy and rebuild the Temple, and invite him to come down from the cross. They don't realize that by not saving his life Jesus is replacing the old Temple with a new Temple not made with hands. Next, the Jewish religious authorities issue the same invitation: "He saved others; he cannot save himself. Let the Christ, the King of Israel, come down now from the cross, that we may see and believe" (15:31-32). They fail to understand that precisely by losing his life and giving it as a ransom for many, Jesus will save those who can believe in a crucified Messiah.

At the sixth hour, that is, at noon, darkness breaks out over the whole land, a symbol that the demonic powers have reached their height and are about to crush Jesus. His encounter with

Satan began in the desert (1:12-13), and it ends with his cry: "My God, my God, why hast thou forsaken me?" (15:34). Engulfed by darkness and overcome by evil powers, Jesus suffers the absence of God. He dies with this cry of weakness and desolation, and he experiences no relief from his enemies. He dies deserted by his followers, taunted by his enemies, derided by criminals, and suffocated in an evil darkness. He even feels abandoned by the God whose will he had accepted in the garden. Bystanders misunderstood his cry as a desperate appeal for help. But Jesus, aware of his struggle with evil, utters another loud cry and breathes his last.

At his death the veil of the Temple is torn, and a Roman centurion confesses him to be the Son of God. The rending of the curtain shows that the Temple has lost its significance as the place of God's presence with his people. Israel's privilege has ended. Now all people, whether Jew or Gentile, have access to the divine presence, not in the Temple but in the crucified Jesus. The Roman centurion faces that crucified Jesus and says: "Truly this man was the Son of God" (15:39). The other soldiers see Jesus' death as another routine crucifixion, but the centurion recognizes this defeated, dead Jew to be the Son of God. In strong contrast to the Jewish religious authorities, in surprising contrast to the absent disciples, this gentile soldier models a faith that finds meaning in the paradox and mystery of the Son of Man dead on a cross. Mark invites us to stand with the centurion and make the same profession of faith.

Women followers of Jesus appear at the foot of the cross. They witness his death, see where he is buried, and come to the tomb on Easter morning to anoint his body. Among his followers, they alone witness his death and burial, and they alone hear the news of his resurrection.

In the absence of the disciples, Joseph of Arimathea, otherwise unknown in the gospel, performs the funeral rites. According to Jewish law, Jesus' body was not to be left overnight on the cross. Joseph receives burial permission from Pilate. A shroud is purchased in haste. But the body is not anointed for burial. The women witness the burial and mark the place so that they might return to complete the ritual begun by the woman at Bethany (14:8-9).

The empty tomb

When the Sabbath rest has ended, the same three women bring spices to anoint Jesus' body, and they go early to visit the tomb (16:1-8). To their surprise the stone is rolled away, and a young man dressed in white is sitting on the side of an empty tomb. Amazed, they do not know what to make of the empty tomb. The young man announces: "Do not be amazed; you seek Jesus of Nazareth, who was crucified. He has risen, he is not here; see the place where they laid him. But go, tell the disciples and Peter that he is going before you to Galilee; there you will see him, as he told you" (16:6-7). He draws attention to Jesus' absence. But he also recalls Jesus' promise that he would go before them to Galilee (14:28). The women are afraid and astonished at the empty tomb and at the young man's announcement of the resurrection. They leave the tomb, but they fail to tell anyone what they have seen and heard. The story ends with their ambiguous and puzzling reaction.

Mark's gospel ends with all that Jesus had predicted about his passion, death, and resurrection fulfilled: betrayal, flight, denial, Jewish trial, mockery, Roman trial, death, burial, announcement of the resurrection. Two other predictions, however, have not been fulfilled. First, at the supper Jesus had told the Twelve that after his resurrection he would go before them into Galilee (14:28). And the women at the tomb hear a young man announce the same news: "He is risen, he is not here; see the place where they laid him. But go, tell his disciples and Peter that he is going before you into Galilee, there you will see him, as he told you" (16:6-7).

The young man's message to the women must have rung in the ears of Mark and his community. His message says more about the second coming of Jesus than about appearances of the risen Lord. For "Galilee" symbolized for them the place where traditional barriers between Jews and gentiles would be broken down. There the Christian community would endure the trials and tribulations that must come before the end. From there they would preach the gospel message to all the nations. In Galilee they would wait with hope for Jesus' coming as the triumphant Son of Man.

In the meantime, Mark and his community experienced Jesus' absence. On the cross Jesus had experienced the absence of his Father. Now in their trials and tribulations, they experience the absence of Jesus. In his death Jesus suffered. They too would suffer abandonment and persecution: in the destruction of Jerusalem and of the Temple, in being opposed and persecuted by the surviving Pharisaic movement. Jesus had passed through suffering and death to the glory of his resurrection and exaltation to the right hand of Power. They too must pass through abandonment before attaining the glory that awaits them when Jesus returns in triumph.

Secondly, at the Jewish trial Jesus had predicted ". . . and you will see the Son of Man sitting at the right hand of Power, and coming with the clouds of heaven" (14:62). Two distinct moments are named—his exaltation and the time of his coming. Exaltation is mentioned here for the first time, but Jesus had spoken earlier about his coming (8:39—9:1; 13:24-27). The gospel does not tell how these predictions are fulfilled. But Jesus' followers and the Jewish authorities are to expect his triumphant return within their lifetimes (9:1; 13:30).

From the passion and resurrection narrative, Mark's readers can be sure that Jesus sits at the right hand of God and will come again just as he predicted. The passion and resurrection narrative demonstrated beyond doubt that Jesus has power to know the future. He had predicted his sufferings and death, and his predictions proved accurate in the least detail. Surely his predictions about being exalted and coming again will also be fulfilled.

Mark's readers, then and now, live between Jesus' announcement that God's Kingdom is at hand (1:14-15) and the time of his final coming in glory (14:62). Mark's gospel, like a novel that ends before the final solution of the plot, closes with a strong message of hope: hope in the midst of hardships and suffering; hope that can survive pessimism about the course of human history; hope in God's kingly power already revealed in Jesus of Nazareth but not yet fully revealed; hope grounded in Jesus' statement to the Jewish authorities: ". . . you will see the Son of Man sitting at the right hand of Power, and coming with the clouds of heaven" (14:62). Jesus' predictions of his passion had already come to pass, and Mark's community experienced the tribulation that must come before the end. So they had every reason to wait and watch in the absence of Jesus and to look forward in hope to the triumphant return of their Lord and Savior, who would establish fully and forever the Kingdom of God.

We conclude our study of Mark with some reflections on how its historical background might resemble our concrete situation in the world and on how Mark's world of images, values, and stories might influence how we live as Christians.

First, when we explored the world behind Mark, we discovered resemblances to our world, which is in a deep cultural transition. Mark dealt with the complex issues that emerged in the postwar reconstruction of Judaism, and we too are dealing with complex changes in the Church and in the secular world. We have seen that the experience of transition, which we share with Mark's community, enables us to enter Mark's world and to learn what it means to live today as Christians.

Second, Mark has invited us into an apocalyptic world of transcendent power. We have studied the symbol "Kingdom of God," the title "Son of Man," and the struggle between good and evil. As Mark's community confronted evil in postwar Judaism, they struggled between hope and despair, power and weakness. We face the same struggle. Do we believe that God's kingly power can still work in our world? Can we imagine a future in which people will live in greater justice, harmony, and peace? Can we choose to live in hope rather than to let despair overwhelm us? Praying with Mark's gospel may not give us easy answers to these questions. But it will give us stories, images of power, and values to help us make meaning in our lives.

Thirdly, we have studied the characters in Mark's gospel, especially those who followed Jesus. We have seen them vacillate between enthusiasm and fear, faith and doubt, understanding and misunderstanding, clarity and ambiguity, fidelity and infidelity. Prior to Jesus' death and resurrection, his followers failed to see the paradox that through suffering he was to enter into his glory. We have recognized that the tensions they experienced can be found in our lives as we witness to the Kingdom. We too find it difficult to accept the paradox in suffering; we shrink from living out that paradox in service to others. But through prayerful participation in Mark we can deepen our commitment to follow Jesus, and we can recognize that no matter what his followers do, Jesus remains faithful in his commitment to them.

Finally, Mark composed his story of Jesus' death and resurrection for a community that keenly experienced Jesus' absence. He had been with them in his earthly life, and he had promised to return soon in glory. Between his departure and return, however, they experienced him as absent and hoped for his return. At times we too may experience Jesus Christ as absent from our world. We perceive no signs of his active presence. As we listen to Mark's message of hope to his community and as we participate in it through prayer, we may begin to see how we might respond to our present tribulations with hope in the kingly power of God.

II

JOHN

5

Getting to Know John's Gospel

Light and Darkness

John sees Jesus as the preexistent Word of God, and he tells the story of Jesus' incarnate life on earth and his return in glory to the Father, which is accomplished through his passion, death, and resurrection. At the same time and at a symbolic level, John's gospel is a story of light encountering darkness. The symbols of light and darkness run like threads unifying the entire gospel. Attention to these two symbols will help you begin to appreciate the gospel message. Two examples from John's gospel will suffice to introduce you to the theme of light and darkness.

At the Feast of Tabernacles, Jesus goes to Jerusalem to participate in Israel's great harvest festival. The Jewish people all gather in the great Temple Court of the Women to celebrate the climax of the festival—the spectacular fire dance. In the center of the court, huge golden menorahs (candelabra), set on bases fifty yards high, burn brightly, shedding light throughout all Jerusalem. Men specially chosen for the occasion enter the spacious court bearing torches. They dance, waving the torches, throwing them into the night sky, and catching them again.

Against this background, Jesus announces to the Jews, " 'I am the light of the world; he who follows me will not walk in darkness, but will have the light of life' " (8:12). In this shocking statement, Jesus confronts his hearers by taking to himself the symbol of light, a symbol rich in tradition and meaning. In proclaiming that the symbol now points to him, Jesus replaces the Jewish festival, and those who choose to follow him as the light will not be caught in darkness but will live in the light.

The following experiment will introduce you to our second example of light and darkness in John's gospel. Imagine you are at a reception in a large room. As you chat with the other guests, the lights suddenly go out and leave you in total darkness. No one has a lighter or other adequate source of light, but the hostess says that she will try to make her way to the basement to find a lantern. Meanwhile, another guest suggests that everyone stay in place and sit down. Being with others makes the darkness more bearable, but you still feel powerless to do anything except hope the hostess will return with the light. Suddenly the door opens, and as the hostess enters with a large, powerful lantern, an intense light floods the room. At first you close your eyes against the bright light, but gradually everyone adjusts to the light's intensity and welcomes the new-found brightness. The hostess sets the lantern down, and all the guests scatter around the room, some nearer the light, some nearer the shadowed dimness.

This experiment in imagination enables us to understand the second image of light, found in the dialogue between Jesus and Nicodemus, a Pharisee and member of the ruling Jewish Sanhedrin. Nicodemus comes by night, that is, in darkness, to ask who Jesus really is. In response to Nicodemus' guarded questions, Jesus explains that out of love for the world, God gave his only Son and sent him, not to condemn the world, but to save it. Eternal life or perdition, approval or condemnation, depends on the decision to believe or not to believe that Jesus is the one sent by the Father. Jesus then concludes his dialogue with Nicodemus with these words:

For God so loved the world
that he gave his only Son,
that whoever believes in him
should not perish
but have eternal life.
For God sent the Son into the world,
not to condemn the world,
but that the world might be saved through him.
He who believes in him is not condemned;
he who does not believe is condemned already,
because he has not believed in the name
of the only Son of God.

And this is the judgment,
that the light has come into the world,
and men loved darkness rather than light,
because their deeds were evil.
For everyone who does evil hates the light,
and does not come to the light,
lest his deeds should be exposed.
But he who does what is true comes to the light,
that it may be clearly seen
that his deeds have been wrought in God. (3:16-21)

Two other passages strongly echo the dynamic of light encountering darkness:

The light is with you for a little longer.
Walk while you have the light,
lest the darkness overtake you;
he who walks in the darkness
does not know where he goes.
While you have the light,
believe in the light,
that you may become sons of light. (12:35-36)

He who believes in me,
believes not in me
but in him who sent me.
And he who sees me sees him who sent me.
I have come as light into the world,
that whoever believes in me may not remain in darkness.
    (12:44-46)

As a bright light dispels darkness, Jesus comes to confront and challenge darkness. He comes, not to judge people, but to elicit a decision for or against the light, a decision by which people judge themselves. As we will see, some will choose to move away from the light and remain in darkness, since the light will make their evil deeds evident. Others will draw close to the light, and as a result they and their good deeds will become more transparent to themselves, to others, and to God. Still others, like the cautious Nicodemus, will for the time being linger at the far edges of the light.

Revelation and Response

The dynamic interaction of light challenging darkness occurs throughout John's gospel, as Jesus reveals himself through signs (actions) and words and as people—both individuals and groups—respond to his revelation. As people respond to his self-revelation, they model various degrees of faith. This interplay of *revelation* and *response* is so basic to understanding John's gospel that it warrants fuller exploration.

To understand this interplay, we can begin by asking, How do we make ourselves known to another person, and how do we respond to him or her? An experience of friendship in my own life will serve to illustrate this process of revelation and response.

Thomas Jacobs, a Jesuit priest, was born in Holland. Since 1949 he has lived in Indonesia, teaching theology in the Catholic seminary, writing articles and books, and conducting retreats and workshops throughout that vast network of islands. Tom and I met in 1963 at the Biblical Institute in Rome, where we had both come to study scripture. We entered the same degree program, attended the same classes, and lived in the same Jesuit community. At first we discussed our intellectual interests, shared our opinions of the classes we attended, and expressed our reactions to the Second Vatican Council then in progress. Eventually we talked about our personal histories and family backgrounds and spent more time together on long walks in the hills outside Rome. Clearly, we were becoming good friends as we attended more carefully to each other's words and actions. As our friendship deepened, we no longer depended in the same way on our words and actions to come to know each other. At a deeper level, we began to know each other as persons, and we began to know ahead of time what the other would say or do. Through the remainder of our student years we shared our lives and our work, and as we did so we grew more united in mind and heart.

In 1966 Tom returned to Indonesia, and I remained in Rome to complete my doctoral studies. Saying goodbye was especially difficult, since Tom and I knew that we might never see each other again. Nor were we sure what effect distance would have on our friendship. Since we could no longer depend on being in the same place at the same time, we had to trust that our friendship would survive the prolonged absence and vast distances that separated us. As it turned out, the separation enabled our friendship to grow in a new way. As time passed, we both experienced a new kind of presence to each other, not a physical presence, but a presence experienced through knowledge and love.

Since 1967, Tom and I have been together on three occasions. Twice he came to the United States for three-week visits, and in 1979 I spent two months conducting workshops in Indonesia. Though we may never see each other again, our friendship remains a strong support in our lives since it has moved beyond physical presence to a presence grounded in the trust that each of us is deeply known to the other and strongly loved.

As I reflect on our friendship and all that it has meant to us, I can better recognize and appreciate the interaction between Jesus and those who came to believe in him as the one sent to reveal the Father. As Tom and I came to know each other by attending to each other's words and actions, so John's Jesus reveals himself to the Jewish people through words and actions. Furthermore, as Tom and I gradually came to discover each other as a person, so too, through Jesus' words and signs, people gradually discovered him as a person, as the Son of God. And finally, just as Tom and I experience each other as present though physically absent, so Jesus' disciples experienced Jesus' presence after he had returned to the Father.

I want now to explore these three distinctive elements—revelation through words and signs, response to Jesus, and Jesus' abiding presence.

As we have seen, Jesus reveals himself as the one sent by the Father through the so-called "I am" sayings. The words "I am," when uttered without a predicate complement, echo the divine name used in the Old Testament: "I am who I am" (Exodus 3:14). John's Jesus proclaims, "Unless you come to believe that I am, you will die in your sins unless you believe that I am he" (8:24). "When you have lifted up the Son of

Man, then you will know that I am he" (8:28). "Before Abraham was, I am" (8:58). "When it does take place you may believe that I am he" (13:19).

At other times, Jesus uses "I am" with an identifying word or phrase drawn from the Old Testament and cherished by contemporary Jews: "I am the bread of life." (6:35,51). "I am the light of the world." (8:12, 9:4). "I am the door of the sheep, . . . I am the good shepherd" (10:7,11). "I am the resurrection and the life." (11:25) "I am the way, and the truth, and the life" (14:6) "I am the vine." (15:1)

The words used here do not define Jesus as he is in himself; rather, they describe his relationship to humankind. In his mission, Jesus is the source of eternal life (vine, life, resurrection). He is the means through which people find life (way, gate). He leads them to life (shepherd). And he reveals to them the truth that nourishes their life (bread).

Jesus also reveals himself through symbolic actions called "signs." "Signs" are miracles that reveal Jesus to have been sent into the world by the Father so that those who believe in him might know the Father. As we have seen in Mark's gospel, Jesus' miracles sometimes dramatize the apocalyptic struggle between God's power in Jesus and the powers of evil in their many guises (possession, disease, storms, death). In John, however, Jesus' seven signs point to Jesus' identity as a person rather than to his power over evil. The first sign at Cana (2:1-11), when Jesus changes water into wine, focuses not on the action itself nor on its material results but on what the miracle reveals about Jesus: (" . . . Jesus manifested his glory; and his disciples believed in him" (2:11). In the second sign at Cana (4:46-54), when Jesus heals the royal official's son, much greater stress is placed on how the official's household came to believe in him than on the action itself.

The remaining signs or miracles are given meaning through Jesus' words. When the words are understood and the sign is seen with faith, they reveal Jesus' person. Each sign becomes the occasion for discussion between Jesus and the person cured or between Jesus and those who witness the cure. That dialogue invites the hearers to recognize that precisely in the sign and in the words Jesus reveals the Father:

- Jesus heals the man at the pool of Bethesda, and the following explanation makes it clear that the healing symbolizes the gift of life (5:1-15, 16-47).
- Later, Jesus multiplies the loaves (6:1-15) and walks on the Sea of Galilee (6:16-21), and the following discourses on the bread of life explain the meaning of the multiplication (6:22-71).
- Still later, Jesus restores sight to the blind man, but the dramatic interchange that follows the miracle shows that Jesus has given him spiritual sight, while the Pharisees have reduced themselves to spiritual blindness (9:1-41).
- Jesus gives life to Lazarus, but his remarks prior to the miracle show that the restoration of physical life is important only as a sign of the gift of eternal life (11:1-44), and the Jewish Sanhedrin condemns him to death (11:45-54).

In reading John, then, we must attend to how Jesus acts, then speaks, acts again, and speaks again. As actions alternate with words, John's Jesus continually challenges and calls his people to recognize and believe in him as the one sent by the Father. In a word, Jesus as light moves through the world of darkness, challenging men and women to decide whether or not to believe in him.

In John's gospel we find a wide spectrum of responses to Jesus. Some refuse to see Jesus' actions as signs or to listen to his words with openness. In John's symbolic language, they refuse the light and choose to remain in darkness (3:19-20). John has Jesus observing that those who reject the light would have been better off had their eyes been physically incapable of sight (9:41, 15:22). Their willful blindness can only be explained as fulfilling the lack of faith predicted in the Old Testament (John 15:25). According to John, those who reject Jesus personify the darkness, and they remain permanently hostile to Jesus the light.

Others see Jesus' signs, listen to his words, and acknowledge him to be a wonder-worker sent by God. Many Jews in Jerusalem, for example, believe in Jesus after seeing the signs he has performed (2:23-25). Nicodemus comes to him at night with these words: "Rabbi, we know that you are a teacher come from God; for no one can do these signs that you do, unless God is with him" (3:2). Such faith is insufficient, however, because it sees Jesus merely as a wonder-worker; it fails to recognize him as the revelation of the Father.

Though some choose not to respond and others respond only halfheartedly, the disciples model Johannine faith. Invited by Jesus to come and see where he is staying, they address him as "rabbi," "Messiah," "son of Joseph," "Son of God," and "King of Israel" (1:35-51). They witness Jesus' first sign at Cana and come to believe in him (2:1-11). After the disciples see Jesus multiply bread and walk on water and after they hear him say, "I am the bread of life" (6:35,48), Peter, their spokesman, professes "Lord, to whom shall we go? You have the words of eternal life; and we have believed, and have come to know, that you are the Holy One of God" (6:68-69). These words show that the disciples have come to know Jesus as the light sent from God and that they stand in that light.

In John's perspective, however, the highest faith is the faith of those who believe in Jesus without being able to see his signs or hear his words, that is, those of us who will read his gospel down through the ages. Such persons grow intimate with Jesus through the gospel account of his signs and wonders; of these people Jesus says to Thomas, "Blessed are those who have not seen and yet believe" (20:29). John then states that he has written his gospel "that you may believe that Jesus is the Christ, the Son of God, and that believing you may have life in his name" (20:31).

At the last supper Jesus gathers with those few who have come to the light and who believe in him as Son of God. Jesus promises that when he has left them to return to the Father, the Paraclete will come to dwell in them so that they will experience his abiding presence even though he is physically absent. Jesus describes the Paraclete, the Holy Spirit, in the last discourses (14:16-17; 14:26; 15:26-27; 16:7-11; 16:12-15). The Paraclete is another Jesus who will come to the disciples only after Jesus has departed. "It is to your advantage that I go away, for if I do not go away, the Paraclete will not come to you; but if I go, I will send him to you" (16:7). Jesus will be with the

Father in heaven, and the Paraclete will fulfill Jesus' promise to dwell within his disciples on earth. Through the Paraclete, both the Father and Jesus will come to the disciples. In guiding and teaching the disciples about Jesus, the Paraclete will be in opposition to the world of darkness. The world of darkness will be put on trial, because it neither sees nor accepts the Paraclete as Jesus present in those who believe.

This view of the Paraclete as Jesus' personal presence in the Christian while Jesus is with the Father characterizes John's view of Christian life. Mark's gospel draws us to look forward in hope to the triumphant return of the Son of Man, but John invites us to grow aware of Jesus' presence now through the Paraclete dwelling within us. We are as near to Jesus' earthly ministry as were the first Christians: The same Paraclete dwells within us as dwelt within them. In reading the beautiful words Jesus addresses to his disciples at the last supper (John 13—17), we see him speaking clearly and directly about his abiding presence with the disciples despite his physical absence. By recalling and disclosing the meaning of Jesus' words and signs, the Paraclete guides God's people in every generation as they face each new situation.

Dramatic Movement

John presents Jesus as the Word that existed with God from eternity, became flesh to dwell among us, and returned to the Father in glory. This dramatic movement can be visualized as a pendulum that swings from God to the world, and from the world to God.

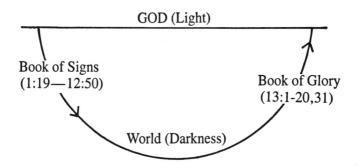

Most scholars call the first half of the gospel the "Book of Signs"(1:19—12:50). Here, we watch Jesus move as light in the world of darkness, calling all persons to judgment—that is, to decide whether or not to believe in him as the one who reveals the Father. In the second half of the gospel, called the "Book of Glory" (13:1-20,31), Jesus instructs his own about discipleship and acts out his love for them by suffering, dying, and rising from the dead. John's gospel ends with an epilogue (21:1-25), an added story about a post-resurrection appearance of Jesus to the disciples in Galilee.

The Prologue summarizes the movement of the whole gospel: "He came to his own home, and his own people received him not. But to all who received him, who believed in his name, he gave power to become children of God" (1:11-12). The "Book of Signs" tells how Jesus came to his own people, the Jews, how again and again he revealed himself to them, and how by and large they failed to recognize him as the revelation of the Father.

The "Book of Signs" is generally divided into four parts. Part 1 (1:19-51) describes the opening days of Jesus' revelation to his own people. It focuses on the testimony of John the Baptist and on how John's disciples come to believe in Jesus.

Part 2 (2:1—4:54) has been titled "From Cana to Cana" because the story begins at Cana in Galilee, moves south to Jerusalem, heads back north through Samaria, and returns to Cana. Within this geographical movement, we see Jesus relate to Jewish religious institutions. He changes the water for purification into fine wine, cleanses the Temple in Jerusalem, and tells the Samaritan woman that he has replaced both Jewish worship at Jerusalem and Samaritan worship on Mount Gerizim. In these chapters individuals and groups react to Jesus and model the spectrum of faith we have already mentioned.

Part 3 (5:1—10:42) is dominated by Jesus' actions and discourses at the great Jewish feasts—Sabbath (5:1-47), Passover (6:1-71), Tabernacles (7:1—10:21), and Dedication (10:22-39). Jesus' words and actions often relate to the dominant images and symbols of the Jewish feasts. For example, he multiplies bread and walks on water at the time of Passover to recall the Exodus symbols of manna from heaven and water from the rock. At the Feast of Tabernacles, with its fire dance and giant candelabra, Jesus announces himself to be the light of the world, and he dramatizes that announcement by curing the man born blind. By taking these symbols to himself Jesus shocks his Jewish hearers into reflecting on his identity.

Part 4 (11:1—12:50) focuses on the theme of life and death, especially in the story of Jesus raising Lazarus from the dead. This section serves as a hinge in the movement of John's gospel. It brings to a close the time of Jesus' self-revelation and begins his movement toward glory. In raising his friend Lazarus from the dead, Jesus initiates the process by which his enemies will put him to death.

The "Book of Glory" (13:1-20,31) describes how Jesus is glorified in his "hour" of passion, crucifixion, resurrection, and ascension—that is, how, through these events, Jesus is lifted up to the Father to enjoy again the glory he had before the world existed. The theme of self-transcending love runs like a thread throughout these chapters. Jesus announces his love for the disciples (13:1). He washes their feet, thus symbolizing the meaning of his passion and death: It will cleanse the disciples and give them a place with him (13:3-20). In the long discourse that follows (13:31—17:26), Jesus commands the disciples to love one another as he has loved them, and he reassures them that in his death he is returning to the Father in glory. He promises that he will return to them after his resurrection, will abide in them through the Paraclete, and will finally come in the parousia. His return will be marked by peace and joy. John then portrays Jesus' passion, death, resurrection, and ascension as a demonstration of self-transcending love, a love-unto-death-for-others that triumphs over death and gives life (18:1-20:31).

Reading John

We have briefly reflected on how the gospel of John is a story of light and darkness, on how Jesus' signs and words reveal his person and invite our response, and on how the narrative's drama unfolds. Now I invite you to set this information aside for the time being and read the gospel in one sitting from start to finish.

As with Mark, I suggest that you read the gospel three times, participating in the text more deeply with each reading. In the first reading, focus on the individual words, phrases, and sentences. Then return to reread, not the whole gospel, but only the sections you liked most and those you liked least. Feel the texture of those sections, whether hard or soft, warm or cold, appealing or repelling. As you read these sections the third time, attend to your response and to the feelings that surface in you as you grow more familiar with the gospel.

I suggest that after you have completed the three readings, you compare this experience with your experience of Mark by doing the following exercise:

1. Select at least three adjectives to complete each of the following sentences, and for each adjective indicate passages in John that support your choice.

   John's gospel is _____, _____, and _____.
   John's Jesus is _____, _____, and _____.
   The relationship between John's Jesus and his disciples is _____, _____, and _____.
   The relationship between John's Jesus and his adversaries is _____, _____, and _____.

2. Think about your response to John, and answer these questions.

   What elements in John (stories, discourses, "signs," passion narrative) did you like most?
   What did you find especially meaningful in John?
   What aspects of John did you ignore?
   What aspects of John did you resist?
   What was your overall reaction to John?

3. Compare John with Mark by answering the following questions:

   What similarities and differences do you see between John's story of Jesus and Mark's?
   What similarities and differences do you see between John's portrait of Jesus and Mark's?

How would you compare and contrast your reaction to
   John with your reaction to Mark?

Now that you have gotten to know John through reading the
text and reflecting on your experience of the gospel, you are
ready to use the gospel for prayer. Our reflections on praying
with John and our suggestions of appropriate methods will help
you use this gospel in prayer.

6

Praying with John

Reflections on Prayer

In describing how to pray with Mark's gospel, we recognized that the desire to pray is a gift from God. When we pray, we respond to that gift by setting aside focused time to be with and to listen to God, and by entering into a loving encounter with God. Similarly, we approach the gospel of John convinced that through prayerful participation in the gospel our relationship with God will deepen and grow.

To enter fully into John's gospel we must recognize that praying with John means letting the gospel function as a story, tale, or imaginative narrative. When we hear a story, we respond to it as story. The meaning of a story unfolds in the telling; we do not go elsewhere to find its meaning, nor do we reduce a story to theory. John tells a story of God's love for the world—a love expressed in sending his only Son as light into darkness. John's story of God's action on behalf of the world is, for those who take it seriously, decisive and of cosmic significance. It influences how they make meaning in their lives. As story, John's gospel has its source in the shared life of a human community. Though it bears the marks of the culture in which it was told and written, the radical truth of the story persists from generation to generation, precisely because all people recognize and experience the story as true. As we will see in studying the world behind John, this gospel had its source in the experience of the diaspora Jewish-Christians recently excluded from the synagogues. As story, John's gospel narrates the primary events that shaped the life of the Johannine community: the life, death, and resurrection of Jesus. John's gospel named the polarities that the community experienced: light and darkness, love and hatred, truth and falsehood. Further, the gospel articulated the hopeful vision of the community becoming children of God.

John's gospel as story, then, constructed and articulated an entire world in which we are invited to live and which we are asked to recognize as our own. John's gospel gives us a landscape rich in imaginative texture and flexible enough to ground us in the past, to help us make meaning in the present, and to provide direction for the future. Today the Christian community prizes the gospel of John because it explains our origins, addresses our present, and envisions our future. In accepting the gospel as a story that constructs our world, we let it show us where we came from, where we are, and where we are going. Ultimately, then, it enables us to decide what is of value in our lives.

John's "world"—rich in symbols, shocking metaphors and disarming irony—demands that we be silent, honest, and open to change. It demands that we be willing to enter John's world and to let ourselves be challenged and confronted by Jesus as we move toward a decision for or against him. Praying with John asks that we be open to symbols such as light and metaphors such as "I am the bread of life." We are asked to be sensitive to the many levels of meaning that the symbols and metaphors carry and to let ourselves be drawn into contact with the transcendent reality they disclose. We are asked to see a truth and to allow it to be in us. We are asked to grapple with the symbols and metaphors, not by pulling them apart with our minds and applying them to our lives, but by simply allowing them to draw us into their world, to let their reality encompass us.

John's gospel asks that we let the light of the symbols and metaphors dawn in our lives just as we let the sun into our lives each morning. To welcome the sun, we must get up early, face east, and wait for the sun to rise. In welcoming John's gospel into our lives, we need to prepare ourselves for prayer by becoming still and by waiting and watching for the gospel's truth and reality to dawn. Though we anticipate the sunrise, we don't thereby cause the day to dawn. Nor do we make the truth of John's gospel dawn in our lives. We simply wait in faith for it to dawn.

Understanding and approaching John's gospel as story and inviting the truth of the gospel into our lives enables us to grow intimate with the risen Lord who is disclosed in John's gospel. The phrase "growing intimate" implies a relationship between persons. "Intimacy" is often understood as a synonym for emotional sharing or sexual expression. However, we use the term more broadly; intimacy is involved whenever we disclose ourselves to another in a personal relationship. In this sense, family and friends are intimate with one another. Also, colleagues and those who share common goals, such as those who share life in religious communities, can also experience varying degrees of intimacy. In a word, intimacy is possible for all who attempt to live closely with others, who share with others their talents and dreams, and who merge their lives and hopes with others.

We are better able to grow in intimacy when we know and accept ourselves while remaining open to new discoveries about ourselves. Self-acceptance and openness to others enable us to be truly empathetic, to modify our responses, to develop tolerance, and thereby to create mutually enriching patterns of behavior. Since in prayer the risen Lord discloses himself to us and invites us to a deep personal relationship, we will use and develop these same resources of awareness and empathy as we grow intimate with the risen Lord whom we encounter in the gospel of John.

But, we might object, the gospel is a written text, and no matter how privileged and unique, the gospel is not another person. How, then, can we grow intimate with the gospel? The text discloses its own world and invites us to find a home in that world. As we prayerfully respond to the gospel, it discloses more of its world to us. At the same time, the gospel challenges us to question or modify our worlds, our views. In this analogous sense, we can speak of growing intimate with the gospel of John.

In a more profound sense, we can establish empathy with the persons we find in the gospel. For example, we can watch the man born blind (John 9), listen to his words, and observe his actions. As we do this, we can enter the scene by identifying with the man or with one of the other characters in the story.

As the characters disclose themselves to us and as we disclose ourselves to them, our appreciation deepens.

We must remember, however, that we approach praying with the gospel of John so that we might grow intimate, not with the gospel nor with its characters, but rather with the risen Lord who reveals himself through the gospel. In praying with the gospel of John we may at times feel overwhelmed by the depth, density, and richness of its world. But if we choose to become absorbed in its truth through imagination, if we surrender the need to control or dissect the gospel, it will open us and stretch us with its truth and the reality it discloses. We must simply receive the gospel and let ourselves be drawn into it. Praying with John means that we enter the gospel story, open and alert to its symbols and metaphors and that we let them work in us and bring us to the person of Jesus. As we cultivate an attitude of stillness and openness, we will be stretched to a greater awareness of the risen Lord who is at work in our lives.

The methods described in the chapter "Praying with Mark" are also useful for praying with John. Some people, however, find that John's gospel is more difficult to read than Mark's gospel. John's story does not move in the same way as Mark's. So the "simple reading" method may not be useful for John's gospel as a whole. Nevertheless, some sections—the Prologue; the stories of Nicodemus, the Samaritan woman, the man born blind, the raising of Lazarus, the trial before Pilate; the last supper discourse; the post-resurrection appearances of the risen Jesus—lend themselves to simple reading.

The "sacred reading" *(lectio divina)* method is suited to both the stories and the discourses. The discourses lead us to ask questions, and once we have begun to understand, a discourse can lead to affective prayer. However, the discourses contain so much material that we are often overwhelmed by the richness of intellectual content. We may find ourselves leaving off point-by-point consideration of the discourses and entering into a simpler prayer in which we attend to the wholeness of the reality disclosed by the text.

The "I am" sayings, which are often found in the discourses, invite us to enter the metaphor. To experience the power of the metaphor "bread of life" in the "I am" sayings, we must engage the metaphor with mind and heart, reason and feelings, intellect and imagination. We then experience its tension, and we remain within that tension until the metaphor cracks open to disclose its deeper truth and hidden reality.

"Sacred reading" may work well with the dramatic stories that invite us to ask about the action, the physical and temporal setting, the words and actions of the characters. For example, we can easily puzzle with Nicodemus, with the Samaritan woman, and the many other characters who misunderstand what Jesus has said to them. And we can let the irony in these scenes lead us to the deeper reality they disclose.

The stories in John's gospel also lend themselves to imaginative contemplation. The seven signs Jesus performs throughout the first part of the gospel are especially suited to imaginative contemplation:

- changing water to wine at Cana (2:1-11)
- curing the royal official's son at Cana (4:46-54)
- curing the paralytic at the pool of Bethesda (5:1-15)
- multiplying the loaves (6:1-15)
- walking on the Sea of Galilee (6:16-21)
- curing a blind man (9:1-41)
- raising Lazarus from the dead (11:1-44)

We can imaginatively create the scene, enter into it, and interact or identify with John the Baptist, Nicodemus, the Samaritan woman, the man born blind, Martha and Mary, Pilate and Thomas. As we talk or identify with these persons, they become real to us. Contemplating them as they meet the Lord can dispose us to encounter the same Lord.

Both "sacred reading" and "imaginative contemplation" may at times seem too busy to be right for praying with John. We may feel drawn neither to meditate on the discourses nor to imagine the scenes. At such times we may simply want to become enchanted with John's story with its symbols and metaphors. We want to move into John's world, which may seem at first like a foreign land. We want to experience that world even if it rubs against, challenges, or even shatters our own world. By praying with John we want to express reverence for his gospel, and we want to make his story our own.

We will now describe two methods especially well suited to praying with John—"prayer with few words" and "prayer with symbols."

Prayer with Few Words

Jack was raised in a Catholic family. His parents sent him to a Catholic grade school and, at some sacrifice, to a strict Catholic high school. His traditional education focused more on moral rules and regulations than on a personal relationship with Jesus Christ. Though he remembered the nuns and priests at school as very strict and distant, they gave him a good education. During his school years, Jack made friends, and others recognized him as a person who always valued his friends.

After high school Jack went to the State university and majored in business and commerce. After graduation and military service, he returned home and eventually married. He and his wife Marcia settled down to begin married life in their hometown. Jack got a job in business, did well at his work, and eventually became manager of his department. He and Marcia saved for a down payment on a small house and began a family. Three babies came at two-year intervals, and Jack and Marcia moved easily and happily into their responsibilities as parents.

As the children reached school age, Jack and Marcia sent them to the local Catholic school. At Marcia's urging, Jack began to get involved in school-related activities. Both were active in their parish; Jack was invited to serve on the parish finance committee, and two years later he found himself on the parish council.

Life seemed to be going along very smoothly. As Jack reached his late thirties, however, four events disrupted his world. At work, Jack began to wonder whether the rest of his life would follow the pattern already established. At this time the eldest son, a sixth grader, was arrested for shoplifting. It took Jack and Marcia some time to realize that their son's petty theft was his attempt to prove to the older boys that he was one of them. Also by this time Jack had gotten deeply involved in the parish.

For the first time in his life, he witnessed dissension that threatened to destroy parish unity. Conservatives and liberals battled about the liturgy. Some parishioners even stopped attending the ten-thirty Mass to avoid exchanging the greeting of peace with people they had fought with at the parish council meeting. Because Jack was so universally well liked, he was often called in to arbitrate parish conflicts. Jack expected conflict in other places, but he thought that he could count on people in the parish being nice to one another. He began to feel that the work he was doing in the parish was the same as what he did at his job, except that he wasn't paid for the thankless parish work.

Meanwhile, Marcia conceived an unplanned baby and had a difficult pregnancy. Most evenings, Jack was out with the other children or was involved with activities at the parish. Jack and Marcia's relationship became strained. They argued much more often. Marcia felt very blue most of the time and seemed to have lost her usual cheerful disposition. Jack felt pressured and annoyed by her complaints about his being out when she needed him at home.

The following Lent, Jack and Marcia decided to attend the Lenten series at the parish. At the third talk, a Cenacle sister quoted a saying from John, "No longer do I call you servants, for the servant does not know what his master is doing. But I have called you friends, for all that I have heard from my Father I have made known to you" (15:15). Jack was struck by the words, and he found them replaying in him as he drove to work, cleaned the garage, or did chores around the parish. As the words came to him, over and over again he intentionally began to entertain them. Almost without his knowing it, a new pattern developed in his life. As he came home from work each day, he kissed his wife and played with the children for awhile. Then he retired to the living room, but rather than pick up the evening newspaper, he sat in his comfortable easy-chair and began to repeat "I no longer call you servant." As Jack moved around to patch up crises at work, in his home, and at the parish, he sensed that he had been feeling like a servant who was living at the edges of this committee work or that conflict situation. He realized his own discontent as he kept hearing "I no longer call you servant." The words began to open up new possibilities.

The next idea also captured Jack: " . . . but I call you friend."
He wanted to hear Jesus address these words to him, and he
began to imagine what it would be like if Jesus Christ were a
real person. In a way Jack never doubted that Jesus was a real
person, but he had always experienced Jesus as a strict and
distant figure telling him what he had to do and ready to judge
him when he went wrong. Jack longed to hear Jesus say, "Jack,
you are my friend." Without knowing it, he simply followed
his heart's desire and asked for the gift of Jesus' friendship.

When Jack went on, "for all that I have heard from my Father
I have made known to you," he began to realize that Jesus had
indeed told him what he had heard from the Father, that his
knowledge was available to him, and that Jesus could be his
friend. Then the entire passage began slowly to change into
words addressed to him personally, "Jack, I don't call you my
servant anymore. I call you my friend, because I tell you who
I am."

Jack slowly began living in these words, and he continued
his ritual of prayer each evening. He received the words and let
them draw him into their reality. Sometimes he brought concerns from work or the parish to his new friend, but most often
he spent time simply being with Jesus.

Marcia stopped complaining that Jack was never around, and
she began to enjoy his quiet presence as she prepared dinner.
Jack and Marcia were more at ease with each other, and their
evenings together were peaceful. Jack's life remained active,
but it became more simple, more quiet, more whole. He felt
rooted in his relationship with Jesus Christ. Jack wanted to
know who Jesus was and what he stood for. He wanted Jesus
to be a person with whom he could talk about the dailiness of
his job or about his work in a parish torn with dissension. In
this relationship with Jesus Christ, Jack found a center from
which to move and to which he could return, a center that brought
him a new sense of peace.

Why was this prayer method so powerful for Jack? He valued
friendship, but his early education did not allow the possibility
of close friendship with Jesus; his strict religious training focused
on moral rules and regulations. Then Jack's adult life grew
frantic with activities. The demands of work and home and the

difficulties in the parish pulled him away from the personal relationships that were central to his life. But when he heard this particular gospel saying, he somehow experienced it as an invitation to friendship with Jesus Christ. This experience profoundly affected everything else—his relationship to his wife and children and to his activities at work and in the parish.

Jack thrived on friendship, so entering into friendship with Jesus naturally appealed to him. As he prayed, his life gradually became integral. Having anchored his spiritual life in Jesus' call to friendship, Jack was able to reestablish his relationships with his wife and children and to responsibly handle his work and the struggles of his parish.

This prayer method is especially recommended, if you, like Jack, wish to learn how to pray with your heart rather than your head. In using this method you are invited simply to say the words to yourself, to form the words by moving your lips or by saying them aloud. Whichever way you choose, repetition is key. Simply repeating the words without trying to understand them enables you to receive them into your heart, to let them become part of the texture of your inner life. As you savor the words you are repeating, as they blend with your life, you may find the sentences transformed to fit your experience, or you may focus attention on one part of the saying. After awhile you may feel deeply nourished by the words. You may then feel drawn to speak spontaneously to the Lord, or you may feel drawn to a loving silence in his presence. In any case, you want to be fully attentive to the Lord you seek.

Prayer with Symbols

At forty-five, Dick to all appearances was enjoying extraordinary success in his work and family. He was married and had four children. Two were in college, and two were finishing high school. As a professor of computer technology, Dick soon became widely recognized for his research and writing, and he was in great demand for lectures to academic and business groups throughout the United States, Western Europe, and Japan. He was the envy of friends, who admired his many achievements as well as the discipline he brought to his work. Dick could sit down and do tough research for long hours without interruption. He solved problems and thought through their implications with creativity and perseverance. He brought the same dogged intensity to his religious duties. He attended church regularly, and he and his wife educated their children to value religion and to develop an intellectual interest in their faith.

But in spite of Dick's successes he felt restless. He knew that he was a good father and that he was widely respected for his work, but he still felt unsettled.

Dick's restlessness came to a head when he was invited to read a paper at a prestigious meeting in computer technology. He had no trouble preparing and presenting a technically sound and well written paper. Afterward, his colleagues congratulated him on his research, but Dick noticed that their praise did not give him the high satisfaction he had experienced on other occasions. He sat through the rest of the conference wondering about the value of all this talk of technology. The flat, gray feeling he was experiencing would not be denied.

More and more, Dick realized that he no longer took time to listen to classical music, to read a poem or a novel, to visit a flower show, sit by the lake, or paint a landscape. In his twenties he had loved all these things, but they had disappeared from his life. He gradually realized that his affective needs, long neglected, were demanding his attention. One day a friend called to tell him about an informal retreat for a small group of men from the parish. Dick liked the men who had organized the retreat, and he thought it might provide an opportunity for him to explore his restlessness, so he accepted the invitation.

The priest who guided the retreat presented reflections based on specific gospel passages. The men reflected privately on the text and then gathered to talk in a group. In the third session, the priest presented a saying from John: "I am the light of the world; he who follows me will not walk in darkness, but will have the light of life" (8:12). He then read a second passage about coming to the light: "And this is the judgment, that the light has come into the world, and men loved darkness rather than light, because their deeds were evil . . . . he who does what is true comes to the light, that it may be clearly seen that his deeds have been wrought in God" (3:19-21).

These passages attracted Dick because he was looking for light to dispel the grayness he was experiencing. He thought about the passages and used them for prayer, letting them become more and more a part of him. Le felt drawn to the light that was Jesus Christ. He began to let the symbol of light shine on his inner darkness. He desired that light, but he also was a little afraid of ᵥ hat he might find at the bottom of his restlessness and afraid of what the light might ask him to change. After considering this attraction and repulsion, he chose to continue being drawn into the light.

Dick used a lit candle to symbolize the choice. As he watched the light push back the darkness in his room, his desire for the light grew stronger. With the candle as a visual symbol of light, he prayed to be drawn more and more into the light that was Jesus Christ. By letting himself be in the light, Dick gradually began to feel more transparent to himself, to others, and to God, and he began to recognize how he had ignored his feelings and affective needs.

As the light began to illumine his life, Dick got more in touch with his feelings and began to reclaim his affective life. People began to notice how he was expressing his feelings more easily, even in his teaching and lecturing. He was less afraid to be transparent with others, and he began to reestablish relationships with his wife and children. Though never a letter-writer, Dick began to write to his son at college. He was amazed at how glad his son was to hear from him and at how good he felt about that. Dick flew out to see his son and to spend a week backpacking with him in the mountains. The two of them began to share what was happening in their lives. Dick also cut back on some of his commitments. As a result, he found life more satisfying, and his restlessness gradually disappeared.

Since the retreat, Dick often uses a candle as a visual symbol of the light that has begun to illumine him and lead him to new life. He prays that the light will continue to shine in his life to dispel the darkness that remains in him. He prays that he might live more fully and more transparently in the light that is Jesus Christ.

Why did praying with the symbol of light prove so effective for Dick? Though he appeared successful, he was restless because his caring heart had been left to lie fallow. The qualities that enabled Dick to be successful—his powers of analysis, his faithfulness to a task, and his strong self-discipline—were the same ones that impelled him to get to the bottom of his restlessness.

When Dick chose the warm glow of the candle to lead him to prayer, he was drawing on his long-neglected affective self. Though the candle focused Dick's attention, it didn't lend itself to analysis nor draw him into reasoning about its meaning. It was for him a rich symbol of Christ, the light who continued to draw him, mind and heart—to awaken his feelings and to fire his imagination. Through the symbol he experienced Jesus Christ. Living in the reality of Jesus the light, Dick felt called, challenged, and empowered to reorder his priorities, to begin to live differently, and to continue to pray by the light that is Christ.

Praying with a symbol means that we let the symbol *as symbol* draw us to the risen Lord. How do we pray with the symbols in John's gospel? There are many approaches to prayer with symbols; I want to describe one approach in six steps. As you enter into prayer, relax your body, empty your mind, and quiet your feelings. In the first step, focus attention on the symbol as a reality outside yourself. In the example given, we attend carefully to the individual parts of the candle—the wick, the flame, the wax. Remain with this step, and with each of the following steps, as long as they hold your attention. In the second step, attend to the feeling tone of the symbol. Is the flame warm or soft, hard or cold, appealing or repelling? In the third step, be aware of how your feelings respond to the symbol. As you draw closer to the light, are you more attracted than repelled, more comfortable with approaching it than worried about getting close? Do you want to turn away?

In the fourth step, let yourself become the symbol. Enter into the light and become absorbed into it until you are one with it and it is one with you. In the fifth step, experience yourself and the symbol becoming one with the whole world. You and the light expand to embrace all men and women, all creation, and you experience all creation as one with yourself in the light. In the sixth step, rediscover your identity within the oneness with all creation. Experience yourself as an individual in union with all creation and within the light that is Jesus Christ.

At any moment in this six-step prayer, the symbol may disclose to you the person Jesus Christ. When that happens, simply move through the symbol to encounter the risen Lord, and remain with him as long as the prayer continues.

The two cases and methods we have described demonstrate once again that praying with John means being open to the risen Lord, being alert to symbols and metaphors through which you can be drawn into contact with the Lord, being willing to participate through feelings and imagination in those symbols and metaphors, and being still enough to grow aware of the risen Lord as he reveals himself in your experience. Through prayer you move into John's story about Jesus. At first that story may seem unfamiliar, strange. It may also rub against, challenge, and shatter your ideas. But as you gradually make John's story your own, you will deepen your relationship with the risen Lord. You will be drawn through John's words, images, symbols, and metaphors to the person of Jesus Christ.

We will now study the gospel of John, its historical background and its story, symbols, and metaphors, so that this study might enrich your experience of praying with John.

7

Historical Background: The World Behind John

As we become more familiar with John's gospel through reading and prayer, we are drawn to ask about its dualism—its way of presenting reality in terms of opposites. We have called the gospel a "story of light and darkness" because the light/darkness dualism runs through the entire narrative. But John reveals a dualistic world view in several other sets of opposites: above/below (8:23), spirit/flesh (3:6), life (eternal)/death (3:36), truth/falsehood (lie) (8:44-45), heaven/earth (3:31), God/Satan (13:27), love/hatred (15:17-18). John's dualism seems more radical ("either-or") than moderate ("both-and") in that Jesus is the light, and those who believe in him live in that light without fear of returning to the darkness. Faced with an "either-or" decision, they have chosen the light, and so they cannot live simultaneously in both light and darkness. John seems to say: "Once in the light, always in the light."

Why is John's world view so radically dualistic? What experience contributed to this view? To answer these questions, we will explore the world behind John, that is, the concrete experience of the evangelist and of his community. As with Mark's gospel, John's gospel originated in a religious milieu quite different from our own. When we acknowledge this difference, we recognize that we must view John's gospel on its own terms and in its own world rather than try to force it into our contemporary world view. Because we know that historical information about John's world will enrich and deepen our religious appreciation of the gospel, we ask: What was the concrete situation of John and his community? How did the gospel come to be? What did the gospel mean to John and his community?

Answering these questions will enable us to appreciate John's gospel in its own environment. We recognize the differences and the distance between the original setting and ours, but we also recognize the similarities that encourage and challenge us to bring our experience into dialogue with that of John's community.

Scripture scholars cannot pinpoint the precise time and exact locale in which John produced his gospel. Most agree that it was written between A.D. 75 and 100. Some scholars hold that the gospel was written at Alexandria in Egypt and Antioch in Syria, but most hold for Ephesus in Asia Minor. Scholars are certain that the gospel was written in dialogue with diaspora Jews—Jews who lived outside Palestine.

Jews in the Diaspora

Archaeologists have found evidence of synagogues, cemeteries, and other identifiably Jewish buildings strewn across the length and breadth of the Roman empire. These findings show that Jews penetrated the Roman Empire to set up diaspora communities. While accurate numbers are impossible to attain, scholars estimate that in the second half of the first century A.D. the total Jewish population outside Palestine far exceeded that of the homeland. Social and economic opportunities (largely trade-related) drew Jewish people away from Palestine.

Charters in the various cities throughout the Empire tolerated associations for work, social purposes, religious identity, commercial business, and the like. This toleration was especially needed, since diverse people brought from their homelands widely divergent backgrounds and interests. Associations were recognized legally even when the members did not possess full rights as citizens. Accordingly, the diaspora Jews secured legal arrangements with Greek leaders and later with the Romans to safeguard their distinctive way of life. With these safeguards, Jews found it advantageous to live as minority groups in the midst of the foreign Greco-Roman culture. In all probability, the legal status of Jewish communities in cities throughout the Roman empire included free association for religious purposes. As a result, the Mediterranean world was dotted with fully organized, quasi-autonomous Jewish communities with their own synagogues and judicial systems.

Inscriptions discovered in various synagogues indicate that a wide range of religious and secular officials sustained the life of the association. At least in some instances, a supervisory group of elders headed by a leader seemed to form the administrative body for several different synagogues with the same city. By way of exception, a few Jews enjoyed civil recognition and positions of honor, both social and administrative.

More significantly, wherever synagogues were established they attracted converts or "God-fearers," that is, those who were attracted to Judaism but who had not undergone circumcision, the formal rite of initiation. Their presence, attributed in part to the missionary activity of zealous Jews, primarily reflects the widespread search for a personal religion in the Greco-Roman world. Simply by living their daily lives, Jews attracted much attention and comment, since their ritualized religion enjoyed a high visibility compared to the informal, occasional practices of civic religions and the secret rites of the mystery religions.

Jews in the diaspora maintained lively contact with the homeland. By imperial decree, they were free to make pilgrimages to the Temple in Jerusalem. And much to the chagrin of local magistrates, they collected and sent abundant offerings with the pilgrims. They built their synagogues facing Jerusalem so that at their Sabbath gatherings they would face the Temple. This orientation toward their native land also made diaspora Judaism distinctive among other religions in the ancient world.

Despite the contact with Palestine, religious attitudes and practices among Jews in the diaspora differed from those of the Jews at home. Diaspora Jews were less concerned for the destiny and fortunes of their native land, since for them the traditional ties between religion and land had been severed. Jerusalem and its Temple remained a central site of pilgrimage and an object of sentimental attachment, but diaspora Jews reevaluated their traditional beliefs about God's unique presence in the Temple. They focused their concern more on individual salvation than on national prosperity. The chief religious figure was no longer the high priest in the Temple who enjoyed religious authority and political power, but rather the synagogue leader, who as prophet and guide interpreted for his community what it meant to live as faithful Jews outside Palestine.

As is generally characteristic of immigrant groups, diaspora Jewish communities tended to cluster in two circles of members. The inner circle was composed of devout, full-time adherents of the Jewish religion as practiced in Palestine. These members normally continued to speak Aramaic (the native language of Palestine). Since they wanted to preserve their traditional values, they avoided adapting to the surrounding majority culture. The outer circle, composed of second- and third-generation immigrants and/or God-fearers—those for whom Judaism was not native—tended to speak Greek rather than Aramaic and thereby initiated a long process of reinterpreting Judaism. The Hebrew scriptures were translated into the Greek Septuagint and were reinterpreted in light of the widely held Greco-Roman ideals and the special needs of diaspora Jewish communities.

This latter group shifted its focus away from a religion based on traditions and customs of their homeland. They were unwilling to depend solely on oral transmission of their traditions from parent to child. Hence emphasis shifted to formulated creeds, law codes, and rules for conversion and admission to the community.

Jews in the homeland inherited their religion as a birthright. Palestinian Jews valued the land to which they had belonged since birth and the Temple in Jerusalem where with their people they worshipped God. Jews in the diaspora, however, cherished their religious traditions out of strong personal conviction, since the surrounding culture tended to challenge rather than support those traditions. Diaspora Jews most likely valued freedom from the homeland. Religion for them transcended the homeland and was independent of any sacred place like the Temple.

The Christian Movement in Diaspora Judaism

Diaspora Judaism, with its right to free association, its protection guaranteed by Rome, and its widespread network of synagogue communities, provided a strong base for Jewish-Christian missionaries as they began to move into the Roman world. The missionary activity of Paul is a case in point. Born a diaspora Jew, Paul first came to know his religion through the local synagogue in cosmopolitan Tarsus. Out of strong devotion to Pharisaic Judaism, Paul later moved to Jerusalem and began to experience his religion in its native place. This exposure gave Paul a strong background for his subsequent Christian mission to Jews and gentiles alike (A.D. 46-58). His strategy was to establish a community in one city and to move on to another center after a relatively short time. He also went first to the Jewish synagogue, where he knew that as a Jew he would always be welcomed. He turned to the gentiles only after the Jews had rejected him. This practice, as he understood it, was in accord with God's plan of salvation—Jews first and then gentiles. Since diaspora centers were not only for Jews but also for gentiles attracted to Judaism, traveling missionaries such as Paul naturally began preaching to these communities in the synagogue as an easy way of contacting both groups. The earliest Christian communities in Asia Minor were established in relationship to synagogue communities, and they understood themselves as strongly related to diaspora Judaism.

We have already seen how the first revolt in Palestine against Rome (A.D. 66-70) created a deep religious crisis for Judaism and for the Christian movement within it. Mark's gospel was written during the transition from a tolerant and pluralistic prewar Judaism to a more restricted postwar Judaism that stressed uniformity, codification, and reconstruction. After the war the Romans could have been expected to ban the Jewish religion altogether. Apparently, Roman authorities were able to distinguish between Jewish political aspirations that they had to suppress in the name of Roman authority and Jewish religious aspirations that they could continue to tolerate.

Rome had always distinguished between Palestinian Jews and Jews in the diaspora. For example, when Titus returned home in triumph after the destruction of the Temple in Jerusalem, he refused to dissolve the rights of the Jewish association in Antioch. This decision illustrates why Judaism was able to survive within the Empire, even when its political ambitions had been thwarted. Roman law continued to guarantee the diaspora Jews the right of free association, and this right provided enough protection for Judaism to survive after the war and even flourish throughout the Empire.

In the postwar period, tension between Judaism and the Christian movement began to mount in the diaspora. The Pharisees introduced measures to identify and ban Christian-Jews from further participation in the synagogues. The Pharisees saw the Christian-Jews as potentially subversive regarding the all-important issue of the Law. In the 80s, attempts were organized to force Christian-Jews out of the synagogues. In the Pharisees' drive to reconstruct Judaism, they initiated formal excommunication as an effective weapon against dissenters.

Late in the first century some Jewish converts to Christianity were formally banned from diaspora synagogues. John's gospel reflects the tension between diaspora Judaism and Christian-Jews recently banned from Jewish synagogues. We see glimpses of this tension in the story of the man born blind (9:1-41). When the Jews interrogate the blind man's parents, John explains their refusal to get involved: "His parents said this because they feared the Jews, for the Jews had already agreed that if any one should confess him to be Christ, he was to be put out of the synagogue" (9:22). This remark reflects the experience of Jewish-Christians in diaspora centers throughout the Roman world. The blind man is a hero and a model for John's community precisely because at the cost of being expelled from the synagogue he continues to believe in Jesus. In his person he acts out the experience of John's community, a community that knew the cost of believing in Jesus.

Of those who would not or could not decide, John comments, "Nevertheless, many even of the authorities believed in him, but for fear of the Pharisees, they did not confess it, lest they should be put out of the synagogue; for they loved the praise of men more than the praise of God" (12:42-43). This editorial comment names a group of Jews who were attracted to Jesus but were afraid to confess their faith publicly lest they be expelled from the synagogue.

In his last discourse, Jesus predicts what John's community was experiencing, "They will put you out of the synagogues; indeed, the hour is coming when whoever kills you will think he is offering service to God" (16:2). John's Jesus sees the hatred of the world for his disciples particularly verified in their expulsion from the synagogue.

From this evidence we can conclude that John wrote his gospel in part to address the tension that had developed between his Christian community and diaspora Judaism. John served a community locked in conflict with the local synagogues. Jewish opposition threatened the Christians, and Christian success in evangelizing Jews and gentiles threatened stability in the synagogues. Each diaspora community, already hard pressed, grew more defensive; each saw the other as its enemy, and dualistic either/or rhetoric began to flourish. Christians, as a minority within the Jewish minority, experienced the world as chaotic, unharmonious, and hostile. They questioned their identity apart from the Jewish synagogues and in the midst of a foreign Hellenistic culture. Merely to survive the ideology of the city and to claim an identity against the synagogue, they gathered in tightly knit, ghetto-like communities.

John taught these communities how they might rebuff the charges made against them by the diaspora Jews. He portrayed Jesus himself as locked in a similar struggle with those Jews who finally had him put to death. And he presented Jesus the person as completing and replacing Jewish Law and worship. John cast his gospel in terms of light and darkness to strengthen and encourage Christians as they struggled to understand the tension between them and diaspora Judaism. Jesus is the light, and whoever believes in him lives in the light. Synagogue officials, like the Jews and Pharisees in the gospel, personify the hostile darkness that cannot overcome those in the light. Christians needed reassurance that the synagogue, with its worship and practices, its social and educational opportunities, was no longer essential to their salvation and that their faith in Jesus as Messiah and Son of God sufficed.

Without forgetting the distance in time and the difference in culture, I would like to suggest some resemblances between John's diaspora situation and our situation as Christians in today's world. We who believe in Jesus Christ may at times feel like diaspora people in the surrounding secular culture. Accustomed to a deep dichotomy between religion and everyday life, between the sacred and the secular, we no longer want to accept that dichotomy by limiting faith to what happens in church on Sunday. We want to live our faith in our family and work situations. We want to respond in faith to the issues and challenges we face, and we want to see in them opportunities to deepen our faith in Jesus Christ. We want faith to pervade our daily lives.

With these desires we may often feel different from most people in our culture. At times we may even be ridiculed for cherishing traditional Christian faith. In the past it might have been culturally, politically, economically, or socially advantageous to believe in Jesus Christ. But the prevailing secular culture tends more to challenge than to support our faith. We have become a diaspora people in our own land. We believe in Jesus Christ more out of personal conviction than conventional birthright, since Christian faith enables us to make meaning in our lives.

As diaspora people, we prudently adapt our faith to the life around us. We learn to bring the occurances of our everyday lives into our prayer and to reflect on who we are in relation to current events. We form communities to share our faith and to give mutual support in living out Christian values. We seek to promote greater justice in the world. Do we not resemble the people in John's community, who, immersed in the pagan Hellenistic world, adapted their faith in Jesus Christ to their lives apart from the Jewish synagogues?

In an increasingly secular world, we who believe in Jesus Christ may at times experience tension and conflict, challenge and even ridicule, from the nonreligious culture. In business, for example, we may feel like foreigners in a strange land when we try to serve others rather than seek money or power for ourselves. We may choose not to worship profit and productivity as our highest values, and we may not want to isolate ourselves from others to get ahead. Since we dare to be different, we may be criticized for choosing to act out of Christian values when they conflict with conventional values. But if we choose to be true to ourselves at whatever the cost, we grow more convinced in our Christian faith. This tension resembles that experienced by Jewish Christians forced to choose between Jesus Christ and conventional Judaism.

Responses to our diaspora situation are like those of diaspora Jewish communities. Some persons want to hang on to traditional values, customs, and practices. For them adapting sensibly to the secular world may mean establishing new practices and cutting out what no longer fits. This group holds that as Christians we may put new life into our traditions, but we must not radically change them. We must stick to the original blueprint. They further argue that change will only unsettle people; it will add to their present confusion, since it seems to betray what we have cherished.

Another group insists that we as Christians in a secular world must not run from the challenges in our present situation. We must not run back blindly into the past nor blindly into a new future. We must learn to live with the tension between traditional Christian faith and our nonreligious culture. We must stay open to the process of adaptation, since through experiencing confusion and ambiguity we will find new meaning in our lives. So, they reason, we must support one another so that we can remain committed in faith to the person of Jesus Christ.

In his gospel, John addressed both the tension that had developed between his community and diaspora Judaism and the challenges involved in adapting to the Hellenistic world. Might John's gospel not also address the tension that we as a Christian minority experience in facing the secular culture in which we live? Might not that very tension strengthen and encourage us as we struggle to make meaning in our everyday lives? With these questions in mind, we go on to describe the world of John's gospel, with its distinctive story about Jesus of Nazareth.

8

John's Story: The Gospel Itself

Portrait of Jesus

Chapter 1 of John's gospel begins with the hymn that acts as a prologue to the entire work (1:1-18). The first chapter then applies a puzzling assortment of titles to Jesus. These titles reveal different perspectives from which people view Jesus at the beginning of his public life—lamb of God, Messiah, the one of whom Moses in the Law and also the prophets wrote, king of Israel, Son of God. The first chapter ends with Jesus speaking of himself as Son of Man.

Referring to Jesus, John the Baptist twice proclaims, "Behold the Lamb of God" (1:29,36). This title evokes a rich assortment of images. First, Jesus is the new passover, the new paschal lamb—God liberating his people from their bondage to sin just as he had liberated the Israelites from slavery. Second, Jesus, like the lamb in Revelation, appears at the end time to destroy all evil in the world (Revelation 5). Third, Jesus, the suffering servant, described as a lamb in Isaiah, atones for the sins of others (Isaiah 53:7). Jesus is sent by God to liberate the world through his life and death. For John, Jesus' death is not so much a sacrifice as a means of glorification and exaltation. We are liberated or saved in knowing and believing in Jesus as a person.

Several titles in John's first chapter have essentially the same meaning: Jesus is Messiah (1:41), the one of whom Moses in the law and also the prophets wrote (1:45), and king of Israel (1:49). In different ways, these titles name Jesus as God's special agent promised in the Old Testament and eagerly awaited by the Jews. The titles mirror Jewish longings, hopes, and expectations for an ideal ruler, a successor to David, who would lead them out of painful submission to Rome, rule them with justice, and establish an era of prosperity, harmony, and peace. He would rescue the Jewish people from economic as well as political oppression. He would correct religious injustices and falsehoods and would destroy the forces of evil in the world. By calling Jesus the Messiah, his followers recognize him to be that ideal ruler come to fulfill their wide-ranging expectations.

But still more, Jesus is "Son of God" (1:34,49). Seen against its Old Testament background, this title may mean simply that Jesus is the anointed king of Israel, the one especially chosen by God. When Nathan speaks to David about Solomon, his son, he conveys God's word: "I will be his father, and he shall be my Son" (2 Samuel 7:14). The title is also applied to the entire people of Israel. Through the prophet Hosea, God refers to them as "sons of the living God" (Hosea 1:10). When Jesus is called "Son of God," the Jews may well have understood the title in its traditional sense as equivalent to Messiah.

In the Hellenistic world, however, the title "Son of God" connoted a divine figure, a divine man especially gifted with powers that have their source in a divine being. Christians adopted the title and applied it to Christ to convey his special relation to God. At the beginning of John's gospel, the title seems to announce overtones of divinity that John expands and develops as the gospel unfolds.

After Jesus has received all these titles—lamb of God, Messiah, the man of whom Moses in the Law and also the prophets wrote, king of Israel, Son of God—he responds to Nathanael's strong profession with this statement about himself, "Truly, truly I say to you, you will see heaven opened, and the angels of God ascending and descending upon the Son of Man" (1:51). Jesus is all that the others have said about him, but what he says about himself both climaxes what they have seen in him and reveals still more about himself: that he is the Son of Man.

Recalling what we said about this title as it appears in Mark, the Son of Man was understood as a special divine agent of God, a heavenly figure in Jewish mythology. He resided with God from creation and would descend from heaven and come among humankind at the end of the present age. He would overcome evil and establish the reign of God upon the earth. A figure whose nature was extra-human, he remains mysterious and hidden until the time when he is to enter human history and bring it to its grand climax. This title on Jesus' lips at the end of a chapter already filled with titles suggests that "Son of Man" most accurately expresses Jesus' true identity.

These accumulated titles indicate that John focuses attention on the person of Jesus as the object of faith. Mark's gospel, as we have seen, is built on the gradual mysterious revelation of Jesus as Messiah and Son of Man. But John's gospel presupposes Jesus' identity as Son of Man. For John, Christian faith is not a matter of coming to acknowledge who Jesus is but of believing in him from the beginning. In Mark, Jesus preaches the kingdom of God, reveals it in his power over evil, teaches about it in parables, and predicts its final coming at the endtime. But in John, Jesus reveals himself in signs and words, inviting people to see and know him and to believe in him as Son of Man and Son of the Father.

John portrays Jesus as fulfilling all expectations of Jews and gentiles alike. If we view John's Jesus from only one perspective, we succeed in catching a glimpse of him, but we fail to comprehend the full reality of his person. Each title, symbol, or metaphor discloses something true about Jesus, but no one of them nor all of them together reveal the mystery of his person. From Chapter 1, John would have us understand that Jesus is the transcendent Son of Man and the universal Son of the Father.

Son of Man

Characteristically, John's gospel announces a title or theme and then develops it through frequent repetition. Jesus announces the title "Son of Man" to his first followers (1:51). Then, allowing pauses for assimilation, the title, like a thread running through a tapestry or a theme recurring in a musical composition, reappears between stories or discourses.

By calling himself Son of Man, Jesus reveals that he originated in a heavenly home and descended into the world below, and once his work on earth is finished he will ascend again to heaven: "No one has ascended into heaven but he who descended from heaven, the Son of Man" (3:13). "Then what if you were to see the Son of Man ascending where he was before?" (6:62). Jesus' descent from heaven is nowhere described within the gospel story, but it is everywhere presumed. All the scenes in the story take place on earth, but Jesus frequently indicates that he really belongs elsewhere and that in the end he will return to his Father in heaven. Since his origin is divine, he does not belong to this world. Jesus appears from somewhere else, stays awhile on earth, but then departs to the place from which he has come.

Throughout the gospel, people often discuss and argue about Jesus' origins. When he claims to be the bread that has come down from heaven, his opponents are puzzled. They know his father and mother. They sarcastically observe that they know where he is from, and his origin clearly isn't heaven (6:42-43). When Jesus speaks of his ascent to heaven, his hearers are further confused. They suggest that perhaps he means he is going to kill himself (8:22). This theme of Jesus as Son of Man descending from heaven, remaining for a time on earth, and then returning to heaven clearly establishes that he originates in another world and truly belongs there.

Jesus reveals himself as the Son of Man most directly and explicitly to the man born blind. The Pharisees claim not to know where he comes from, while the man born blind comes to recognize that he is from God (9:29,33). At the climax of the process by which the blind man comes to faith, "Jesus heard that they [the Pharisees] had cast him out [of the synagogue], and having found him he said, 'Do you believe in the Son of Man?' He answered, 'And who is he, sir, that I may believe in him?' Jesus said to him, 'You have seen him, and it is he who speaks to you.' He said, 'Lord, I believe,' and he worshipped him" (9:35-38). The blind man comes to the full light of faith in responding to Jesus' revelation of himself as the Son of Man.

Jesus also speaks of himself as Son of Man and to his death as his "glorification." "The hour has come for the Son of Man to be glorified. . . ." (12:23). "Now is the Son of Man glorified, and in him God is glorified" (13:31). These sayings strongly state that Jesus' death may look like defeat but that in fact it is his triumphant glorification as Son of Man.

Jesus expresses the same irony when he speaks of being "lifted up": "And as Moses lifted up the serpent in the wilderness, so must the Son of Man be lifted up, that whoever believes in him may have eternal life" (3:14-15). The Greek word for "lifting up" can mean the act of crucifying, that is, lifting a victim up onto the cross, but it can also mean the act of exalting or honoring a person. When Jesus speaks of his death as his being lifted up as the Son of Man, he suggests both meanings: In the very act of being raised up on the cross he will begin his ascent to the Father.

Elsewhere he says that when he is lifted up, his true identity will become clear, and his departure to his heavenly home will be accomplished: "When you have lifted up the Son of Man, then you will know that I am he, and that I do nothing on my own authority but speak thus as the Father taught me" (8:28). "The crowd answered him, 'We have heard from the law that the Christ remains forever. How can you say that the Son of Man must be lifted up? Who is this Son of Man?' Jesus said to them, 'The light is with you for a little longer. Walk while you have the light, lest the darkness overtake you. . . .While you have the light, believe in the light, that you may become sons of light'" (12:34-36). As we will see later, these sayings announce the irony in Jesus' passion and death: It is his triumphant glorification.

Son of the Father

Readers of John's gospel often ask about the relationship between Jesus and the Father, between Jesus and God. Is he subordinate to, or equal to, God? Most often, he seems subordinate. As God's agent in the world, he obeys his Father, serves his will, and enjoys close personal intimacy with him. "My food is to do the will of him who sent me, and to accomplish his work" (4:34). "The Son can do nothing of his own accord, but only what he sees the Father doing; for whatever he does, that the Son does likewise. For the Father loves the Son and shows him all that he himself is doing" (5:19-20). "I can do nothing on my own authority. . . .I seek not my own will but the will of him who sent me" (5:30). "For I have come down from heaven, not to do my own will, but the will of him who sent me" (6:38). "As the Father sent me and I live because of the Father . . ." (6:57). "My teaching is not mine, but his who sent me" (7:16). "I do nothing on my own authority but speak thus as the Father taught me. And he who sent me is with me; he has not left me alone, for I always do what is pleasing to him" (8:28-29). " . . . for I proceeded and came forth from God; I came not of my own accord, but he sent me" (8:42). "We must work the works of him who sent me, while it is day" (9:4).

These passages describe a heavenly being who descended to earth to carry out the Father's will by teaching and challenging persons to the same obedience, and by dying and rising from the dead. John's Jesus is obedient, subordinate, subservient, even obsequious. He draws strength from his intimacy with the Father, and the Father supports and sustains him. "My Father . . . is greater than I" (10:29). "I live because of the Father" (6:57). "The Father has sent me" (5:36; 6:57; 8:16). As the ever-obedient agent and messenger, Jesus walks the earth with calm assurance and security against his enemies.

Elsewhere in the gospel, however, we are surprised to find that the reason for Jewish hostility against Jesus is that he "made himself equal with God" (5:18). Again, we read: "'I and my Father are one.' The Jews took up stones again to stone him. . . .The Jews answered him, 'We stone you for no good work but for blasphemy; because you, being a man, make yourself a God'" (10:30-32). The Jewish accusation was that he claimed to be a divine being equal to God.

Jesus also claims for himself God's divine power to raise the dead. "For as the Father raises the dead . . . and gives them life, so also the Son gives life to whom he will" (5:21). Jesus demonstrates that power most forcefully in raising Lazarus from the dead (11:1-53). He announces that he is the one who on the last day will raise those who believe from the dead (11:25-26), echoing a refrain from the discourses on the bread of life (6:39,40,44,54).

Similarly Jesus claims for himself the divine power of self-resurrection. "For as the Father has life in himself, so he has granted the Son also to have life in himself" (5:26). Jesus demonstrates this claim when he speaks about raising himself from the dead. "For this reason the Father loves me, because I lay down my life, that I may take it again. No one takes it from me, but I lay it down of my own accord. I have power to lay it down, and I have power to take it up again; this charge I have received from my Father" (10:17-18). The New Testament writings usually refer to Jesus as raised from the dead by the mighty hand of God. But here Jesus says he will raise himself from the dead; thus he claims for himself a power elsewhere reserved to the Father.

In John's gospel, then, two distinct threads are woven into a single tapestry. First, Jesus claims that he is God's agent in the world, that he is sent by and is obedient to his Father. Second, Jesus claims that God has given him rank, status, and power equal to himself. Thomas' profession of faith reflects this claim— "My Lord and my God!" (20:28). The evangelist wants his readers to imitate this faith and repeat this profession. John leaves his readers with the implicit invitation to make this faith our own.

Through these different facets, John presents a portrait of Jesus that we can best describe as incarnational; that is, it claims that Jesus existed with God prior to his appearance on earth, became fully human in his birth, life, and death, and returned to his home with God when his work on earth was finished. Jesus in John's gospel is at the same time human and divine, at home on earth and a stranger to this world. John's incarnational portrait of Jesus can be visualized as shown on p. 130.

John's portrait of Jesus reflects and speaks to the needs of his community. As Jewish leaders forced Christian Jews away from conventional synagogue life, community members focused on Jesus as their leader and guide. He was a messenger from heaven who came to reveal the Father and show them how to live in the Hellenistic world. Though human like themselves, John's Jesus was also the transcendent Son of Man and the Son of the Father, who fulfilled and replaced the traditional Jewish symbols, rituals, and institutions. Those who believed in Jesus

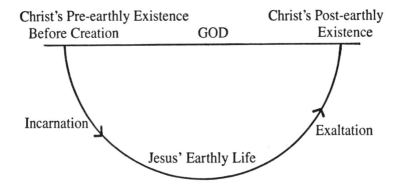

Christ's Pre-earthly Existence / Before Creation — GOD — Christ's Post-earthly Existence

Incarnation — Jesus' Earthly Life — Exaltation

were assured that he would show them the way to God and enable them to become children of God.

In closing our consideration of Jesus as John beautifully and powerfully portrays him, we turn again to the hymn about the Word that stands as the Prologue to the gospel.

In the beginning was the Word,
and the Word was with God,
and the Word was God.
He was in the beginning with God.

All things were made through him,
and without him was not anything made.
That which has been made was life in him,
and the life was the light of men.
The light shines in the darkness,
and the darkness has not overcome it . . .

He was in the world,
and the world was made by him,
yet the world knew him not.
He came to his own home,
and his own people received him not.
But to all who received him,
who believed in his name,
he gave power to become children of God . . .

And the Word became flesh,
and dwelt among us, full of grace and truth;
we have beheld his glory,
glory as of the only Son from the Father . . .
And from his fulness have we all received,
grace upon grace

John 1:1-18

Characters and their Faith Development

As we have seen thus far in our study of John, faith means coming to know Jesus as the revelation of the Father and acknowledging him to be Messiah and Son of God. Those who were impressed with Jesus' signs and who believed in him as a wonder-worker were not yet people of faith. To believe in him means to see beyond words and actions to the person and to recognize that person as a man from God. Those who refused to be open to his words and actions chose, in effect, to remain in darkness (9:41). Others merely acknowledged Jesus as a wonder-worker sent from God (2:23-25), but the disciples believed in him at Cana (2:11) and came to know him as the Holy One of God (6:68-69).

Throughout the gospel we meet other characters who model the faith process: John the Baptist (1:19-36; 3:22-30), Nicodemus (3:1-21; 7:50-51; 19:39), the Samaritan woman (4:4-42), the man born blind (9:1-41), Martha and Mary (11:1-44), Pilate (18:28-19:22), and Thomas (11:14-16; 14:5; 20:24-29). Now we will look carefully at these characters, at how they respond to Jesus and his revelation, and at what we might learn about faith from their response. In so doing, we will find ourselves in these characters and see resemblances between their faith and ours.

John the Baptist, a man strongly aware of his identity, knows his role in God's plan of salvation, fully accepts its limits and responsibilities, and never pretends to claim more for himself. In the Prologue, the evangelist identifies John as one sent by God to bear witness to Jesus the light, so that through his witness all might come to believe. He is not the light, but he comes

-131-

to bear witness to the true light that is coming into the world (1:6-8).

The evangelist develops John's mission at the beginning of the gospel. When the Jews send priests from Jerusalem to ask John about his identity, John disclaims that he is the Christ, Elijah, or the prophet. Only then does he positively assert, "I am the voice of one crying in the wilderness, 'Make straight the way of the Lord,' as the prophet Isaiah said" (1:23). John's disclaimers serve as a foil to the positive identification of Jesus, since what John denies about himself is later shown to be true of Jesus.

John speaks of Jesus as the one who comes after him, the thong of whose sandals he is not worthy to untie (1:27) and as a man who ranks before him (1:30). And when John sees Jesus, he acts out his role as witness to the light: "Behold, the Lamb of God, who takes away the sin of the world" (1:29,36). He identifies Jesus as the one who rights the world's wrongs and breaks the commanding power of sin and darkness.

The Baptist also discloses that God revealed Jesus as the Messiah and Son of God, the servant and Messiah on whom God's spirit rests. Jesus fulfills the divine promise that characterizes the messianic time when God would pour out his Spirit to cleanse and sanctify his people, to bring them true knowledge and make them holy (Isaiah 32:15-16; 44:3-5; Ezekiel 36:25; Joel 2:21-29).

When Jesus returns the next day, John the Baptist again points him out to his disciples. They then leave John to become Jesus' disciples (1:35-36). John fulfills his role of bearing witness to all men and women, including his own disciples.

Later in the gospel, the evangelist presents Jesus and John with their disciples baptizing in the same general area (3:22-30). When asked about the crowds going to Jesus for baptism, John reiterates that he is not the Christ and that he has been sent before Jesus as the groom's best man whose duty is to arrange for the wedding. Now that he has prepared the bride—the People of Israel—for Jesus the messianic bridegroom, John fades into the background with dignity. For his hopes have been fulfilled with the coming of Jesus the Messiah, whose presence causes him true joy. John's last words in the gospel reflect his awareness of his role in God's plan for salvation: "He must increase, but I must decrease" (3:30).

Later, Jesus describes John as a man in whom the Jews rejoiced, "a burning and shining lamp" (5:35) who bore witness to the truth. But Jesus' own testimony is greater than that of John (5:36). Finally, Jesus returns to the place where John first baptized. When people come to see Jesus, they reflect, "John did no sign, but everything that John said about this man was true" (10:41). Even in John's absence, his witness continues to influence the Jews and leads many of them to believe in Jesus.

John models faith for us all, because as believers we are called to witness to Jesus the light. He saw Jesus as Messiah and Son of God. He disclaimed all other roles, and through his words and actions he faithfully witnessed to Jesus. Once the people, including his own disciples, came to believe in Jesus, John withdrew, content that his mission had been accomplished. We learn from John the Baptist that faith includes the call to witness to Jesus as light in a world of darkness. With John we accept our role as witnesses in God's plan of salvation. With John, we claim nothing more and pretend no less than meeting the demands of being witnesses. In our everyday lives, through our words and actions we follow Jesus and believe in him. Like John the Baptist, we acknowledge that we are to point the way so that others might come to know Jesus as the Son of God.

Nicodemus, a Pharisee and member of the Jewish Sanhedrin, represents a small group of Jewish leaders who hesitantly risk believing in Jesus. He approaches Jesus under cover of night's darkness and expresses a partial faith basec on the signs Jesus has performed. "Rabbi, we know that you are a teacher come from God, for no one can do these signs that you do unless God is with him" (3:2). The dialogue moves in typically Johannine fashion. Jesus attempts to raise Nicodemus' consciousness with a challenging statement about becoming born again, from above (3:3-4), but Nicodemus misunderstands because he cannot see beyond the physical realities of everyday life. Jesus offers a clarification, but it leads only to further incomprehension (3:5-10). Jesus then speaks of himself as the Son of Man who travels in an arc from glory to glory, and he points out the personal conviction involved in one's judgment for or against the light (3:11-21). As the dialogue ends, Nicodemus seems to vanish into the darkness from which he came, apparently none the wiser, his faith no more mature.

The perception of Jesus' signs, even without seeing what they really signify, leads Nicodemus to hear Jesus' revealing word. But despite his willingness to come to the light, Nicodemus does not perceive that light very clearly. He seems hesitant and unable to make the decisive step from darkness to light by rising to a faith that rests on the word Jesus speaks to him. Later in the gospel, he seems to grow in faith. For at a moment of intense conflict among the Pharisees, Nicodemus speaks out on behalf of Jesus: "Does our law judge a man without first giving him a hearing and learning what he does?" (7:51). Later we see Nicodemus acting openly as a faithful follower as he arranges an honorable burial for Jesus (19:39). Through conflict with his fellow Pharisees and after Jesus has been lifted up on the cross, Nicodemus moves into the light.

What can we learn about faith from Nicodemus? He shows us, first of all, that faith based on the wonderful signs which Jesus has performed is an acceptable first stage. But mature faith must be centered on the person of Jesus, Messiah and Son of God. Like Nicodemus, we can perceive in Jesus' words no more than their literal meaning. We can fail to respond to Jesus' challenge by refusing to let ourselves be drawn through his words to his person. Jesus tells Nicodemus and us that if we want the Kingdom we must be reborn, that if we want to come into the light and be saved we must act in truth. We alone have responsibility for the choice. For judgment consists in preferring to remain in darkness (as did Nicodemus initially) rather than choosing to come to the light. Jesus offers Nicodemus and us an adult faith, a faith grounded more in personal conviction than in external authority and convention, a faith based on personal knowledge of Jesus Christ as Messiah and Son of God.

In contrast to the Pharisee Nicodemus, an unnamed *Samaritan woman* dramatizes the struggle experienced in rising from the things of this world to faith in Jesus as the Messiah (4:4-42). We are invited in this story to reflect on the Samaritan woman—who she is and who she becomes. As a woman with many husbands, she lives separate from the other women; as an outcast, she cannot associate with other women nor accompany them to the well at sundown, the customary time for drawing water. So she comes alone in the noonday heat to draw water from Jacob's well. Jesus, wearied from the heat, rests alone at the well as the woman approaches. He asks her, "Give me a drink" (4:7). With his request, Jesus, the light, breaks through the racial, social, and economic barriers that separate Jews from Samaritans, men from women. Men did not initiate conversations with women in public, nor did Jews initiate conversations with Samaritans, whom they considered heretics. The woman, surprised by Jesus' request, responds, "How is it that you a Jew, ask a drink of me, a woman of Samaria?" (4:9). With these words she begins an encounter with the light that will lead her to faith in Jesus as the Messiah.

In the dialogue that follows, Jesus issues a challenge: If she recognizes who is speaking to her, she will ask him for living water (4:10). But the woman misunderstands; she thinks that Jesus is referring to the water at the bottom of the well. "Sir, you have nothing to draw with, and the well is deep; where do you get that living water?" (4:11). When Jesus explains that he means the heavenly water of eternal life, the woman asks for the water without fully understanding what she is requesting (4:13-15). She has nevertheless taken a significant step toward the light.

Again Jesus confronts her, but this time his challenge concerns her personal life: "Go, call your husband, and come here. . ." (4:16). Earlier, the woman chose to encounter the light. But now that light begins to penetrate the dark corners of her life as Jesus tells her everything she has done. "You are right in saying, 'I have no husband'; for you have had five husbands, and he whom you now have is not your husband: this you said truly" (4:17-18). Again she must decide whether to turn her back on Jesus or to remain in the light. Will she pick up her bucket and walk back to the city, or will she remain in dialogue with Jesus at the well? For the Samaritan woman this is the critical moment of judgment, of decision for or against the light. The woman responds, "Sir, I perceive that you are a prophet" (4:19). She chooses the light, even though her evil deeds have been exposed. And in the process she recognizes Jesus to be a prophet.

As the dialogue continues, Jesus invites her to still greater faith. She begins to associate him with her people's messianic expectation. "I know that Messiah is coming (he who is called Christ): when he comes, he will show us all things" (4:25). Jesus responds with a simple, direct self-revelation: "I who speak to you am he" (4:26). Through his challenges and her misunderstandings, the woman has been tested and has remained open to the gradual revelation of Jesus, the light. Now she is prepared for Jesus' word that reveals him to be the long-awaited Messiah.

Jesus' disciples return to interrupt his dialogue with the Samaritan woman, and they marvel that by speaking with her he has violated important Jewish customs. The woman runs off to the nearby city to share her enthusiasm for Jesus. When she communicates her experience to the townspeople, she stresses the personal challenge in Jesus' words. This woman of ill repute assumes the unlikely role of missionary to her people, but she still hasn't come to fully believe in him as the Messiah. "Come, see the man who told me all that I ever did. Can this be the Christ?" (4:29).

Meanwhile at the well, Jesus speaks to his disciples about their mission (4:31-38). He tells them to lift up their eyes and see that the fields are white for the harvest. They see ripened fields, but they also see a new harvest—the Samaritan towns-people coming toward Jesus. The Samaritan woman who leads them models the mission Jesus had just described to his disciples.

The Samaritan townspeople at first come to believe in Jesus on the woman's testimony. But when he accepts their invitation to remain with them for two days, they come to know Jesus through his words and actions. Once the Samaritan woman had brought them into the light, her work as intermediary was finished. The Samaritans respond to the light with the striking profession of faith: "We have heard for ourselves, and we know that this is indeed the Savior of the world" (4:42).

What can we learn about faith from this encounter between Jesus and the Samaritan woman? What patterns might we expect to see repeated in our faith experience? Jesus lives, understands, and continually reveals a heavenly reality different from the woman's earthly reality. He doesn't abandon his reality to enter into hers; rather, he invites her through challenge and confrontation to rise to his world view. Teaching the Samaritan woman in stages, he attempts to take her from where she is to a higher level of awareness about himself as Messiah and Son of God. At times this same pattern of challenge and consciousness-raising may be verified in our experience as Jesus invites us into his reality, his view of the world.

The Samaritan woman wins our admiration because she remains open to Jesus' revealing word even when she does not understand. In her we see the dynamic process of coming to faith. She inquires about rather than dismisses Jesus' word. At painful moments she chooses to remain in the light rather than to return to the darkness from which she has come. She first addresses Jesus as "sir"; later she recognizes him as a "prophet," and finally, she strongly suspects that he is the "Messiah." In her process of coming to faith she also witnesses to her fellow Samaritans by sharing her experiences. Overcoming whatever shame she might feel, she points Jesus out to them, invites them to come and see the man who had told her everything she had done, and then withdraws so that the Samaritans themselves might come to know and believe in Jesus. Her faith moves her to minister to others.

The Samaritan woman's struggle to rise from the things of the world to faith in Jesus models a process that can help us recognize our own experience of coming to know Jesus and to ask him for living water. Like the woman, we are invited to remain true to our process of faith as we reach out to share our experience with others so that they, too, might encounter the light that can transform their lives.

The *man born blind* models a faith that develops through conflict with conventional Jewish authorities and withstands expulsion from the Jewish synagogue. In spite of overwhelming obstacles, the man born blind comes to the strong conviction that Jesus is from God, and he receives from Jesus the revelation that Jesus is indeed the Son of Man. In contrast, the Jewish Pharisees model unbelief; by insisting that they already see clearly, they remain blind to Jesus' person, and they gradually sink deeper into darkness.

The man born blind from birth knows only darkness until he encounters Jesus, the light of the world. Jesus spits on the ground and makes clay of the spittle. The blind man feels Jesus put clay on his eyes and hears him say, "Go, wash in the pool of Siloam (which means Sent)" (9:7). Still walking in darkness, the man goes and washes, and he comes back seeing the bright light of day for the first time.

With his physical sight restored, the formerly blind man faces a series of interrogations in which he describes his cure and makes statements that reveal his ever-deepening knowledge of the man who restored his sight. The man knows what he has experienced, and he will not let others deny it. But at first he does not know any more about Jesus than what the cure revealed. The subsequent interrogations force him to reflect more deeply on the meaning of his cure, and he gradually comes to recognize that the man called Jesus is a prophet and a man from God.

Through conflict with the conventional religious authorities, the Pharisees, the man becomes convinced that Jesus is from God. In their initial interrogation, the Pharisees are certain that Jesus is not from God, since he fails to observe the Sabbath. The blind man describes his cure. "He put clay on my eyes, and I washed, and I see" (9:15). In response to their hostility he admits ignorance about whether or not Jesus is a sinner. But as the conflict continues he recognizes Jesus as a prophet (9:13-17).

In a final confrontation, the Pharisees repeat their conviction that Jesus is a sinner, and once again the blind man disclaims all knowledge about that point. He knows only that though he was blind, he now sees (9:25). The Pharisees wonder where Jesus has come from, and the man born blind marvels at their stupidity. He reasons, "We know that God does not listen to sinners, but if any one is a worshiper of God and does his will, God listens to him. Never since the world began has it been heard that anyone opened the eyes of a man born blind. If this man were not from God, he could do nothing" (9:31-33). At that, the Pharisees throw him out of the synagogue. Throughout this heated conflict, the man stands firm and defends his experience, reflects more deeply on the meaning of his cure, and comes to a deeper insight about the person who cured him. Far from shattering his faith, the conflict with official Judaism has enabled the man to become convinced that Jesus is from God.

In a final dramatic scene, Jesus finds the man and reveals that he is the Son of Man:

> Jesus heard that they had cast him out,
> and having found him he said,
> "Do you believe in the Son of Man?"

> He answered,
> "And who is he, sir,
> that I may believe in him?"

> Jesus said to him,
> "You have seen him,
> and it is he who speaks to you."

> He said,
> "Lord, I believe."
> And he worshiped him. (9:35-38)

As with the Samaritan woman, Jesus reveals himself to the man only after testing him through questioning and conflict. That self-revelation climaxes a process of moving from physical blindness to spiritual sight. The blind man encountered the light, and his physical sight was restored. Through the interrogation, hostility, and conflict that lead to his expulsion from the synagogue, the man born blind moved toward spiritual sight as he recognized that his physical cure revealed the man called Jesus to be a prophet and a man from God. The man's fidelity to his experience prepared him to encounter the light, that is, to believe in Jesus and worship him as the Son of Man.

The Pharisees offer a striking contrast to the man born blind. They act as if they see everything clearly, yet they move more deeply into blindness. In their first interrogation, some seem to accept the man's story about his healing; others are offended at the Sabbath violation, and still others seem open to the blind man's evaluation of Jesus (9:13-17). In the next scene they attempt to discredit the story by questioning the man's parents about their son's blindness (9:18-23). In their final encounter, the Pharisees seek to trap the man in the details of the cure (9:24-34). Refusing to accept Jesus as sent by God, they expel the man from the synagogue and thereby plunge themselves into darkness. Jesus makes clear that the Pharisees who sit in judgment against the former blind man actually judge them-selves by failing to recognize Jesus as the light of the world.

As we saw in the last chapter, the Johannine communities were largely made up of Jewish converts who, like the blind man, had been banned from the synagogues. The man born blind was their hero and model of faith because, through con-flict with conventional religious authorities, he became more deeply convinced that Jesus was a man from God. His story taught them that by standing firmly in their faith and by re-maining faithful to their experience, they would grow in their conviction that Jesus is the Son of Man and the Son of the Father.

We too find the man born blind an attractive model of faith. Like the Samaritan woman, he teaches us that faith demands that we be ready to move from blindness to sight, from darkness to light. The man born blind shows us that our original expe-rience of Jesus grows precisely through fidelity to that experi-ence. For as believers, we must be ready to be tested through encounters with friends and enemies alike. We must expect our faith to grow toward conviction through conflict and opposi-tion. But fidelity in the midst of conflict will lead us, as it led the man born blind, back to Jesus to hear him reveal his true identity. With the man born blind we will bow down at Jesus' feet in worship.

Martha and Mary, sisters of Lazarus who was raised from the dead, model two different styles of responding to Jesus (11:1-44). Martha is more thinking, verbal, active, and practi-cal, whereas Mary is more feeling, nonverbal, passive, and intuitive. When Jesus comes, Martha rushes out to meet him, but Mary remains sitting quietly at home until she hears that the teacher has asked for her. Then she rushes out to him and falls at his feet (11:29,31-32). Jesus recognizes the uniqueness of each woman and communicates accordingly. He responds to

Martha verbally, but he and Mary communicate through unspoken feelings. By his sensitivity to each of them, Jesus shows a fully human love for Martha and Mary.

Martha meets Jesus with an implicit request: "Lord, if you had been here, my brother would not have died. And even now I know that whatever you ask from God, God will give you" (11:21-22). Jesus talks to Martha and explains the meaning of the sign he is about to perform for Lazarus. He refers to the sign by saying that Lazarus will rise, but Martha understands him to be expressing the customary comfort by referring to the final resurrection (11:23-24).

Jesus then announces that he is the reality that conquers physical death. "I am the resurrection and the life; he who believes in me, though he die, yet shall he live, and whoever lives and believes in me shall never die" (11:25-26). What Martha expects to happen on the last day is realized in the present. Though physical death is the common lot of all persons, faith in Jesus gives eternal life. Martha professes faith in Jesus, but she doesn't refer to Lazarus: "Yes, Lord; I believe that you are the Christ, the Son of God, he who is coming into the world" (11:27; see 20:31 also). Though a woman of faith and trust, Martha does not yet see Jesus as having the power to give life. Later at the tomb, the thinking, reasonable Martha raises a practical objection against taking away the stone and in so doing reveals once again that she does not expect Jesus to raise her brother from the dead (11:38-40). Through her dialogue with Jesus, we see that Martha has recognized him to be an intermediary heard by God, but she has failed to recognize that he is the resurrection and the life.

When Mary receives word that the teacher is calling for her, she rises quickly and goes out to him. She sees Jesus and falls at his feet. This gesture expresses both her grief for Lazarus and her reverence for Jesus. She addresses the same words to Jesus as did Martha. "Lord, if you had been here, my brother would not have died" (11:32). But her implicit request invites a much different response. Her words, actions, and tears communicate her deep feelings of sorrow and grief for her brother, and Jesus responds with equally strong feelings. He is deeply moved and troubled in spirit, and he weeps for his beloved friend Lazarus (11:33,35,38). Moved by sorrow, Jesus goes to the tomb, orders the stone removed, prays to his Father, and commands Lazarus to come out (11:38-44). Lazarus does come forth, and Jesus gives orders to unbind him.

In our relationship to Jesus, we, like Martha and Mary, are meant to be our truest and most honest selves. Martha did not pretend to be Mary, nor did Mary pretend to be Martha. In meeting the Lord in prayer, we do best to find a style of prayer suited to our temperament and to our present needs. Meditation will be more suited to times when we want to reason and ask questions, to consider causes and draw conclusions, to see the logical links between events or actions. At other times we may find imaginative contemplation better suited to our needs— when we want to see a single event in its concrete reality, enter into it, and get a feel for the actual experience. This story tells us that we can come to know the Lord by reasoning with our minds as Martha does or by trusting our feelings in Mary's way. Jesus met and communicated with each woman without demanding that she be someone other than herself. With the same sensitivity, Jesus comes to meet us as we are at the moment.

Pilate models a person who fails to decide for or against the light. Though convinced of Jesus' innocence, he is unable to act on his conviction. Because Pilate will not choose between Jesus and those who represent darkness, he ends up capitulating to the Jews and handing Jesus over to them to be crucified.

We can imagine the story of Pilate as a drama staged with two sets—one, the outside court of the praetorium where the Jews are gathered, and the other, the room inside the praetorium, where Jesus is held prisoner. In seven carefully balanced scenes, Pilate moves back and forth to address the Jews outside and to talk with Jesus inside. Inside, the atmosphere is calm and quiet; Jesus stands secure in his authority and in full command of the situation. Outside, the crowds with frenzied shouts of hatred pressure Pilate to find Jesus guilty. Pilate's nervous movement from one setting to the other mirrors the struggle taking place within his soul.

Pilate tries to win his way without making a clear decision about Jesus, but in the process he gradually loses all authority to decide Jesus' innocence or guilt. Ironically, Pilate's certainty about Jesus' innocence increases at the same rate as the political pressure to put him to death. Pilate first attempts to dismiss the case by telling the Jews to judge Jesus themselves according to their law, but the Jews insist that he must decide (18:31). After interviewing Jesus, Pilate announces that he finds no crime in him. However, instead of using his authority to release Jesus, Pilate appeals to his custom of releasing one man at Passover. The Jews thwart his plans when they exhort the crowds to cry out, "Not this man, but Barabbas!" (18:40). Pilate next attempts to free Jesus by having him punished by the Roman soldiers, who scourge and mock him as king of the Jews. Pilate then brings Jesus out to the Jews, repeating that he finds no crime in him, but the Jews demand that he be crucified (19:4-7). Still struggling to release Jesus, Pilate brings him out a second time, and the Jews cry out, "Away with him, away with him, crucify him!" (19:15). When Pilate asks if he should crucify their King, the Jews respond, "We have no king but Caesar" (19:15). Pilate finally abdicates all responsibility and hands Jesus over to be crucified.

It seems that the Jewish authorities have condemned Jesus to death, but in fact they have condemned themselves by refusing to accept the light. What appears to be the trial of Jesus before Pilate is in fact the trial of Pilate before Jesus. Only in the end does Pilate take a stand against the Jews. When they complain about the title "King of the Jews" that he has put on the cross, Pilate asserts, "What I have written I have written" (19:22).

John presents Pilate as a person to be pitied rather than hated. In so doing, John invites us to recognize the Pilate in ourselves, the person at times caught between light and darkness, unwilling to make a clear choice. At such moments we lose our rightful power and find ourselves unable to stand with conviction in the light. Not sure of our faith in Jesus as Son of Man and Son of God, we feel confused inside, as though darkness had overcome the light. Like Pilate, we vacillate, unable to decide between Jesus the light and the forces that press us toward darkness. At times, Pilate's trial is the trial of anyone who chooses to believe in Jesus.

Our last character, *Thomas the Twin,* models the faith that grows through misunderstanding, doubt, and cynicism. Thomas first appears in the gospel as Jesus is about to go to raise Lazarus from the dead. Jesus says that for his disciples' sake, he is glad that they were not there when Lazarus died, so that they might believe through the sign he would perform. Thomas responds only to the inherent danger in going to Bethany, which is near Jerusalem, "Let us also go, that we may die with him" (11:14-16). Clearly misunderstanding Jesus' meaning, Thomas assumes that nothing is going to happen regarding Lazarus and that death is all that awaits the disciples. So with a certain pessimistic enthusiasm, he shows himself willing to follow Jesus even to death.

At the last supper, Jesus announces that he goes to prepare a place for the disciples and that he will come again to take them to himself. He tells them that they already know where he is going, but Thomas objects: "Lord, we do not know where you are going. How can we know the way?" (14:5). Jesus then clearly explains that he is going to the Father and that he represents the way to the Father. "I am the way, and the truth, and the life; no one comes to the Father, but by me" (14:6).

After the resurrection, Thomas is not with the other disciples when Jesus appears and gives them the Holy Spirit. On hearing the news about the Lord's appearance, Thomas responds with doubt, even cynicism. He then sets down clear conditions to be met before he will believe their story. "Unless I see in his hands the print of the nails, and place my finger in the mark of the nails, and place my hand in his side, I will not believe" (20:25). Eight days later Jesus again appears to the disciples, and Thomas is with them. Jesus does not rebuke Thomas for his lack of faith; rather Jesus does precisely what Thomas had demanded—he asks Thomas to see the prints of the nails, to place his fingers on the mark of the nails and his hand in Jesus' side. Jesus meets Thomas precisely in his cynicism and doubt and invites Thomas to faith. Thomas responds with the strongest profession in the gospel, "My Lord and my God!" (20:28). Thomas the doubting cynic has become Thomas the believing follower.

We can easily identify with Thomas, since at times we find ourselves more doubting than faith-filled, more misunderstanding than understanding, more cynical than trusting. Jesus comes to us, just as he came to Thomas—not to rebuke us but to meet us in our experience and to respond to our demands. From Thomas' struggles we learn that attitudes that seem opposed to faith can lead to deeper faith in Jesus as Lord and God.

John has written his gospel for us—the silent audience seated in the darkened theater, an audience that has viewed the dramatic action between Jesus and the characters we have seen. As the curtain begins to fall and the house lights come up, Jesus turns to us, the body of believers, the group that has participated in the action on stage. The words he addresses to Thomas apply to us too: "Have you believed because you have seen me? Blessed are they who have not seen yet believed" (20:29).

Faith, then, is ultimately what matters, whether or not that faith comes from seeing Jesus. Thomas' faith depended on touching Jesus' hands and side, but Jesus praises the still greater faith of all who, in his physical absence, never see or touch him but who come to believe in him through the testimony of others. John wrote his gospel "that you may believe that Jesus is the Christ, the Son of God, and that believing you may have life in his name" (20:31). Through prayerful participation in the gospel, especially through interaction with the characters and their faith development, we can dispose ourselves to grow in the faith announced by the evangelist.

The following six statements summarize John's portrayal of faith development in the characters we have studied.

First, faith means encountering Jesus and letting him raise our awareness to the spiritual realities he reveals.

Second, faith is a response to God's gift. In Jesus, God offers us a choice to move toward or away from the light.

Third, we look primarily to our own life experience, not to authorities outside our experience, to find the meaning of our faith.

Fourth, faith grows through conflict and challenge, if we stand within our experience and refuse to allow others to pressure us to deny our experience.

Fifth, faith is a *process* of coming to recognize Jesus as the one sent by the Father, as the Messiah and Son of God. As a process, faith leads us through a misunderstanding or a vague understanding to deeper levels of awareness about Jesus.

Sixth, faith includes witnessing to others by making our experiences available to them and by inviting them to encounter the light so that they might believe in Jesus.

John's portrayal of faith development encouraged his community members in their struggle to find meaning in their lives. John urged them to see their faith as a dynamic process within their experience of being a minority in the Hellenistic world. Though they were expelled from diaspora Judaism, they were to stand firm in the conflicts with the synagogues, were to understand the conflicts as strengthening their faith and deepening their conviction. Above all, they were to recognize Jesus as the light at the center of their lives, and they were to ask him to lead them to a deeper faith. John's view of faith also encourages us as we raise similar questions about what it means to be Christians in the modern world.

Jesus' "Hour of Glory": Encouragement for Believers

The movement in John's gospel is summarized in the Prologue: "To his own he came, yet his own people did not receive him" (1:11). As we saw in the "Book of Signs" (1:19—12:50), when Jesus came to his own, for the most part they failed to believe in him. Now, in the "Book of Glory" (13:1—20:31), we will see how Jesus empowers those who believe in him to become God's children, as the Prologue summarizes: "But to all who received him, who believed in his name, he gave power to become children of God" (1:12).

The introduction to the "Book of Glory" announces the dominant theme of Jesus' "hour": "Now before the feast of the Passover, when Jesus knew that his hour had come to depart out of this world to the Father, having loved his own who were in the world, he loved them to the end" (13:1). Jesus' "hour" is the time of his passion, crucifixion, resurrection, and ascension—the time in which he loves his own unto death and is lifted up to the Father to enjoy the glory he had before the world began (18:1—20:31). Jesus' "hour" is also the time of the last supper, when he gathers his own to wash their feet, to predict Judas' betrayal, to instruct his disciples on what it means to be the children of God, and finally, to pray to his Father (13:2—17:26).

Last supper

John's narrative of the last supper begins with the scene of Jesus washing the feet of his disciples, an action that anticipates both the last discourse and the passion-resurrection narrative. To understand the significance of this action, we must first appreciate how it reverses conventional Jewish hospitality. According to custom, the Jewish host or hostess provided water for guests to wash their feet, which would be heavily soiled from traveling the dusty roads of Palestine. Each person washed his or her own feet, and though disciples occasionally washed their master's feet as a sign of their devotion, no one was expected to wash another's feet. Even slaves were free of this requirement of washing the feet of their masters.

So when Jesus, the disciples' lord and master, chooses to wash their feet, he humbles himself and freely takes on the form of a servant. Jesus' action demonstrates a complete self-giving love; it also symbolizes his passion and death, because it anticipates the total expression of Jesus' love—his death on the cross.

Jesus' action is simple and direct: He rises from table and lays aside his outer garment, girds himself with a towel, and pours water into a basin. He then begins to wash his disciples' feet and wipe them with a towel. At first Peter resists, but Jesus tells Peter that by refusing to accept this act of love, he cuts himself off from him. "If I do not wash you, you have no part in me" (13:8). For the foot-washing clearly points to Jesus' passion and death, and in insisting that they accept this menial service, Jesus prepares Peter and the disciples to accept the same gift of self-sacrificing love. Conversely, not accepting the foot-washing means refusing to accept salvation through participating in Jesus' suffering and death. When Peter sees what is at stake, he expresses characteristic enthusiasm. "Lord, not my feet only, but also my hands and my head!" (13:9). Peter allows Jesus to serve him and thereby comes into communion with Jesus. The full meaning of having Jesus wash his feet will unfold after Jesus' passion and death are accomplished.

Jesus further interprets the foot-washing by telling his disciples, "If I then, your lord and teacher, have washed your feet, you also ought to wash one another's feet. For I have given you an example, that you also should do as I have done to you" (13:14-15). Jesus, their rabbi, has performed for his disciples an act of service that generous disciples might occasionally do for their rabbi. Surely the disciples ought to do similar acts of service for one another. The love and service expressed in Jesus' foot-washing must characterize the disciples' love and service. They are to continue Jesus' mission of self-giving and humble service. Jesus' example leaves no doubt that his followers must be willing to carry their love for one another to the point of laying down their lives.

After washing his disciples' feet, Jesus prepares the disciples for his imminent departure and instructs them about what it means to become children of God.

The last discourse also explains the significance and the implication of Jesus' return to the Father. By anticipating the coming events, Jesus' discourse prepares the disciples to understand the meaning of his passion and death. Throughout the gospel, Jesus has addressed largely hostile audiences against a background of rejection by the world. Now at the last supper, he speaks directly and intimately to "his own," that is, to those whose feet he has washed and for whom he is about to lay down his life.

The disciples have come to believe in him and have become aware of his relation to the Father. Now he instructs them about their identity as his followers and teaches them how to be true followers. Their identity is determined by their relationships with one another, with Jesus in his physical absence, and with the world. They are to love one another with a self-sacrificing love modeled on Jesus' love for them. They will receive the Paraclete, who will dwell in them to guide them and to teach them about Jesus. And they will experience permanent hostility from the world of darkness. These relationships will identify them as a community of those who believe in Jesus. Jesus' instructions are meant to strengthen the disciples in his absence and to help them maintain their identity even under difficult circumstances.

Jesus' command that his disciples love one another echoes and develops his words to them after washing their feet, "You ought also to wash one another's feet" (13:14). The love he commands is further elaborated in the following passages:

A new commandment I give to you,
that you love one another;
even as I have loved you,
that you also love one another.

By this all men will know
that you are my disciples,
if you have love for one another. (13:34-35)

As the Father has loved me,
so have I loved you;
abide in my love.

If you keep my commandments,
you will abide in my love,
just as I have kept my Father's commandments
and abide in his love. . . .

This is my commandment,
that you love one another,
as I have loved you.
Greater love has no man than this,
that a man lay down his life for his friend.
15:9-10,12-13

Clearly, the love which unites the Father to the Son and the Son to his followers must find concrete expression in the disciples' love for one another. Loving one another means obeying Jesus' commands, and obeying Jesus' commands means loving one another.

The disciples cannot earn or achieve such love apart from God. The ability to love is a pure gift passed from the Father to the Son and from the Son to those who believe in him. The disciples' love for one another extends and continues both God's love for the world, which is revealed in sending his only Son, and Jesus' love for them.

In commanding his followers to love one another, Jesus does not exclude those outside the community. In fact, outsiders will recognize in the disciples a love distinguished by self-sacrifice and obedience, a love that can only be from God. This transcending love will continue Jesus' own mission to be a light in the world of darkness. The disciples' love confronts those outside the community and invites them to come to the light. This description of love as the identifying quality of the community was especially meaningful to Johannine communities, since they were separated from their Jewish roots and were unsure of their identity as Christians. Jesus' message to them, "All men will know that you are my disciples, if you have a love for one another" (13:35), establishes for them a new and lasting identity.

Along with the command to love, Jesus promises that when he has returned to the Father, the Paraclete will come to dwell in them, empowering them to experience his own abiding presence even in his physical absence. Jesus will remain with them through the Paraclete whom he will send to guide them and teach them all truth. The Paraclete dwelling in them will enable them to carry out Jesus' command by guiding and teaching them about Jesus. And this will happen within their lifetimes. The following passages describe the Paraclete's role in relation to the disciples and to the world.

And I will pray the Father, and he will give you another Paraclete, to be with you forever, even the Spirit of truth, whom the world cannot receive, because it neither sees him nor knows him; you know him, for he dwells with you, and will be in you. (14:16-17)

But the Paraclete, the Holy Spirit, whom the Father will send in my name, he will teach you all things, and bring to your remembrance all that I have said to you. (14:26)

But when the Paraclete comes, whom I shall send to you from the Father, even the Spirit of truth, who proceeds from the Father, he will bear witness to me; and you also are witnesses, because you have been with me from the beginning. (15:26-27)

Nevertheless I tell you the truth: it is to your advantage that I go away, for if I do not go away, the Paraclete will not come to you; but if I go, I will send him to you. And when he comes, he will convince the world of sin and of righteousness and of judgment: of sin, because they do not believe in me; of righteousness, because I go to the Father, and you will see me no more; of judgment, because the ruler of this world is judged. (16:7-11)

I have yet many things to say to you, but you cannot bear them now. When the Spirit of truth comes, he will guide you into all the truth; for he will not speak on his own authority, but whatever he hears he will speak, and he will declare to you the things that are to come. He will glorify me, for he will take what is mine and declare it to you. All that the Father has is mine; therefore I said that he will take what is mine and declare it to you. (16:12-15)

At Jesus' request and in Jesus' name, the Paraclete will come from the Father. He can come only when Jesus has departed, and he guarantees Jesus' abiding presence when Jesus is physically absent. The Paraclete fulfills Jesus' promise that he will dwell with his disciples. The disciples will be granted the privilege to know and to recognize the Paraclete, since he will be within them and remain with them. He will guide the disciples along the way of all truth by teaching them and disclosing to them the things to come. He will glorify and bear witness to Jesus, but the world will not see, know, or recognize the Paraclete. Against the setting of the world's hatred, the Paraclete will prove the world wrong about its judgment of Jesus.

This portrait of the Paraclete as the abiding presence of Jesus reveals a distinctive understanding of the Christian life. In Mark, Jesus addressed the question of his return by predicting a time of intense suffering and tribulation and by describing a vision of the Son of Man coming in triumphant glory (13:1-37). Mark's readers experienced this tribulation and Jesus' absence in postwar Judaism. They found meaning in Jesus' instructions to endure the suffering, carry out the mission to all nations, and patiently await his imminent return.

By contrast, John's gospel records Jesus' words about the Paraclete and thereby reassures the disciples and all Christians in their struggles. What had been predicted about Jesus' return in glory—judgment of the disciples and the world, the gift of divine sonship, eternal life—is already present in the abiding Paraclete. They can look within themselves as individuals and as communities and can discover Jesus as the Paraclete already present in their midst.

In the last discourse Jesus also warns his disciples that they can expect to experience a permanent hostility from "the world," that is, the darkness over against which they, like their master, must stand.

> If the world hates you,
> know that it has hated me
> before it hated you.
> If you were of the world,
> the world would love its own;
> but because you are not of the world,
> but I chose you out of the world,
> therefore the world hates you.
>
> Remember the word that I said to you,
> "A servant is not greater than his master."
> If they persecuted me,
> they will persecute you;
> if they kept my word,
> they will keep yours also.
>
> But all this they will do to you on my account,
> because they do not know him who sent me. (15:18-21)
>
> I have said all this to you
> to keep you from falling away.
> They will put you out of the synagogues;
> indeed, the hour is coming
> when whoever kills you will think
> he is offering service to God.
> And they will do this

because they have not known the Father, nor me.
But I have said these things to you,
that when their hour comes
you may remember that I told you of them. (16:1-4)

In his desire to encourage his disciples, Jesus describes how the world of darkness will be directed against them just as it was directed against him and the Father. Since the disciples have been chosen to be his friends and have been taken out of the world and called to live a life of faith and love, they will encounter the same rejection as he has encountered. Those who "hate" the disciples ultimately reject God's own revelation in Jesus. The world's hatred for the disciples is manifest in its refusal to accept Jesus, and this refusal establishes a conflict as irreconcilable as the conflict between light and darkness.

Hatred based on unbelief characterizes the world, just as love based on faith characterizes the community of disciples. Jesus leaves the disciples in the world, even though they do not belong to the world. By communicating Jesus' word through preaching and teaching, they will bear witness to him as the light of the world. In so doing they will stand in absolute contradiction to the world of darkness; and as aliens in the world, they can expect to provoke trouble. For, like Jesus, they are sent not merely to change but to challenge the world and to separate the children of light from the children of darkness.

As the last discourse had foretold, the disciples did experience persecution from religious and civil authorities alike. The Jews resented the name "Christ" by which the disciples professed Jesus as Messiah, the anointed one. The Christians' use of this revered Old Testament title gained for them expulsion from the synagogue. The Romans resented their claim that Jesus is "Lord," a title reserved for the Roman Emperor. The Johannine communities recognized in these conflicts the persecution Jesus had predicted, for the abiding Paraclete enabled them to recall Jesus' words and to apply them to their situation. Similarly, Jesus speaks through the Paraclete to all Christians and assures them that he is present despite his physical absence.

The image of a vine and its branches expresses the close identity of Jesus, the Father, and the disciples:

I am the true vine, and my Father is the vinedresser. Every branch of mine that bears no fruit, he takes away, and every branch that does bear fruit he prunes, that it may bear more fruit. . . .As the branch cannot bear fruit by itself, unless it abides in the vine; neither can you, unless you abide in me. I am the vine, you are the branches. He who abides in me, and I in him, he it is that bears much fruit, for apart from me you can do nothing. . . .By this my Father is glorified, that you bear much fruit, and so prove to be my disciples. As the Father has loved me, so have I loved you; abide in my love. If you keep my commandments, you will abide in my love, just as I have kept my Father's commandments and abide in his love. . . .This is my commandment, that you love one another as I have loved you. Greater love has no man than this, that a man lay down his life for his friends. You are my friends if you do what I command you. . . .This I command you, to love one another.

(15:1-2,4-5,8-10,12-14,17).

Jesus later prays to his Father that his disciples throughout the ages might share in the oneness they enjoy with each other. Such oneness comes from both Father and Son, and it draws the believers into a unity with the Father and Son and with one another:

I do not pray for these only,
but also for those who believe in me
through their word,
that they may all be one;
even as thou Father art in me,
and I in thee,
that they also may be one in us,
so that the world may believe
that thou have sent me.
The glory which thou hast given me,
I have given to them,
that they may be one
even as we are one,
I in them and thou in me,

that they may become perfectly one,
So that the world may know
that thou hast sent me
and hast loved them
even as thou hast loved me. (17:20-23)

Passion-Resurrection narrative (18:1—20:31)

Jesus speaks of himself several times as the Son of Man ascending into heaven; he claims that his death, which may look like defeat, actually initiates his triumphant glorification (12:23; 13:31). In fact, when Jesus is lifted up, his identity will become clear, and his glorification will be accomplished (8:28; 12:34-36). The glory normally associated with the resurrection, ascension, and sending of the Spirit is already present in Jesus' suffering and death.

John frequently uses the word *hour* to designate this significant period in Jesus' life—the hour of his return to the Father (13:1). After the Sanhedrin has decided to kill Jesus, and Mary has anointed him for death, Jesus comes to Jerusalem in triumph. When the gentiles come to see Jesus, he indicates that God's plan of salvation has begun to unfold and that his hour has come (12:23). He is certain that the hour is at hand, since God's plan cannot be accomplished except through his passion and death, his resurrection and ascension.

In contrast to Mark, whose message is that Jesus must pass through suffering to glory, John collapses the sequence of suffering and glory into one single "hour of glory." John tells the story of that hour of glory in a narrative that includes the same elements we have seen in Mark—the arrest in the garden (18:1-11), the Jewish trial and Peter's denial (18:12-27), the Roman trial before Pilate (18:28-19:16), the execution on the cross and the burial (19:17-42), the empty tomb and the appearances of the risen Lord (20:1-31).

The Jesus who comes at last to his hour differs from the Jesus of Mark's passion narrative. John portrays Jesus conscious of his preexistence and therefore conscious that his death is a return to the Father (17:5). Jesus is not a victim at the mercy of his opponents, since he has freely chosen to lay down his life with utter certitude that he will take it up again (10:17-18). Though some struggle remains in John's narrative of the passion, we are not kept in suspense about its outcome, since the satanic prince of this world has no power over Jesus (14:30). Indeed, Jesus has already conquered the world (16:33) and, as ominiscient, cannot be caught off guard by events that occur in the passion (2:25; 6:6).

At his *arrest in the garden*, for example, Jesus is not surprised by Judas and the arresting party, as he was in Mark's account (18:1-11). Rather he goes forth to meet Judas, whom he has been expecting. Ironically, Judas, who has aligned himself with the forces of darkness, comes equipped with lanterns and torches. When he left Jesus at the supper, darkness truly reigned (13:30); now Judas needs artificial light to carry out his decision to betray the true light who has come into the world.

The Jesus who confronts Judas is not the Jesus we saw in Mark, who had been prostrate in the dust of Gethsemene praying that his hour and the cup of suffering might pass. Since he and the Father are one, the Jesus of John's gospel rejects any prayer that the Father save him from this hour (12:27). Judas, the Roman soldiers, and the Jewish police lie prostrate in the garden—not Jesus. The representatives of worldly power, both civil and religious, are struck down when Jesus announces "I am he" (18:6). Clearly, no one can take Jesus prisoner nor take his life from him unless he permits it (10:18). Though they have no power over Jesus, these soldiers and police do have power over his own who remain in the world (17:15). Jesus exhibits the care that he expressed at the last supper (17:9-11); he protects them by asking that they be released (18:8).

The *Jewish trial* of Jesus is not the formal procedure before Caiaphas the high priest that we saw in Mark's gospel. Rather, Jesus faces a police interrogation before Annas, Caiaphas' father-in-law. This investigation attempts to uncover sufficient evidence of revolutionary behavior (18:19). Supplied with such evidence, the high priest would then be able to determine whether Jesus was to be handed over for trial by the Romans. In this interrogation, a supremely self-confident Jesus easily outpoints Annas (18:20-21); as a result, his captors are enraged to the point of striking him (18:22). Jesus then asks, "If I have spoken wrongly, bear witness to the wrong; but if I have spoken rightly, why do you strike me?" (18:23).

While Jesus is testifying to his innocence, *Simon Peter is denying him* (18:15-18,25-27). Peter's denials frame the interrogation before Annas and heighten the contrast between master and disciple. Peter denies that he was ever in the garden and that he is a disciple of Jesus. In contrast, "another disciple," known to the high priest, enters the court and persuades the maid to let Peter into the high priest's court. This "disciple whom Jesus loved" appears frequently during the hour of Jesus' return to the Father. He is present at the last supper (13:23-26), at the court of the high priest (18:15-16), at the crucifixion (19:26-27), at the empty tomb (20:2-10), and at certain appearances of the risen Jesus (21:7,20-23). In each scene, the unnamed disciple is introduced as a foil to Simon Peter, and he is portrayed in a more favorable light than Peter. He is a trustworthy and reliable eyewitness to Jesus' hour of glory, a patron and hero for the Johannine community.

John's scenario for *the Roman trial* is a much more polished creation than the Markan scenario . John choreographs an elaborate drama, with the priests and the crowd outside the praetorium, Jesus inside, and Pilate shuttling back and forth between the priests and the crowd (the darkness) and Jesus (the light). The trial develops in seven carefully balanced scenes.

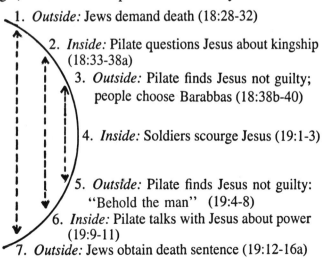

1. *Outside:* Jews demand death (18:28-32)

　2. *Inside:* Pilate questions Jesus about kingship
　　(18:33-38a)

　　3. *Outside:* Pilate finds Jesus not guilty;
　　　people choose Barabbas (18:38b-40)

　　　4. *Inside:* Soldiers scourge Jesus (19:1-3)

　　5. *Outside:* Pilate finds Jesus not guilty:
　　　"Behold the man" (19:4-8)

　　6. *Inside:* Pilate talks with Jesus about power
　　　(19:9-11)

7. *Outside:* Jews obtain death sentence (19:12-16a)

Jesus' few words to Pilate reveal him as an enigmatic figure, a man of power and mystery. Jesus answers the charges of political complicity. He does not refuse the title "King of the Jews," but he states that his real reason for coming into the world was not to assume political leadership but to bear witness to the truth (18:37). As we have seen, Jesus' eloquence and self-assurance challenge Pilate to accept Jesus as the truth. But Pilate, like a chameleon, takes on the different colors of the parties who engage him. Jesus calmly tells Pilate that he may think he has power over his life but that in reality he has no independent authority. Jesus does not fear Pilate; Pilate fears Jesus. The real question is not what will happen to Jesus, since he controls his own destiny, but whether Pilate will condemn himself by acceding to the will of the people. Though convinced of Jesus' innocence, Pilate fails to exercise his power to release Jesus. By failing to make a clear decision, he gradually loses all power to decide whether Jesus is innocent or guilty, and he hands Jesus over to be crucified.

John's account of *the execution and burial* of Jesus focuses on six short scenes. Like a TV cameraman, John simultaneously zooms his camera lens in on Pilate and the title on the cross, the Roman soldiers and Jesus' garments, Mary and the disciples whom Jesus loved, the dying Jesus, the piercing of his side, and the removal of the body and preparation for burial (19:17-42). John shows how these six scenes reveal the meaning of Jesus' death on the cross.

In the first scene, the inscription "Jesus of Nazareth, King of the Jews" is fastened to the cross as a proclamation to the entire world. At the trial, Pilate presented Jesus to his people as a king, only to have him rejected. In these important languages of the Empire—Hebrew, Latin, and Greek—Pilate now reaffirms Jesus as King of the Jews. This official representative of the greatest political power on earth, the Roman Empire, ends up announcing for every passerby to see that Jesus reigns in glory from the cross.

The second scene describes the division of Jesus' garments. Here John explicitly alludes to Psalm 22:18 and pays particular attention to the seamless tunic that was not divided (19:23-24). John's free interpretation of the Psalm 22 highlights the tunic and associates it with the seamless tunic of the high priest, as if to suggest that Jesus on the cross is not only a king but also a priest. This theme of Jesus a priest reflects his prayer at the last supper: "And for their sake I consecrate myself, that they also may be consecrated in truth" (17:19).

In the third scene, women appear at the foot of the cross. Both John and Mark mention the women, but only John includes the mother of Jesus and the beloved disciple (19:25-27). These two persons, mentioned by title and never by name throughout the gospel, meet for the first time at the moment of Jesus' death. In this scene their historical identity is far less significant than what they symbolize. Mary symbolizes much more than her physical relationship to Jesus as his natural mother. Jesus announces a new relationship in which his physical mother assumes a role as spiritual mother of the beloved disciple, and the disciple assumes a role as her spiritual son. Thus as Jesus is about to die, he creates the community of disciples with Mary as its mother and the beloved disciple as its symbolic representative. Jesus is concerned to the end for his own, for those who will be drawn to him now that he has been lifted up from the earth (12:32). Jesus may seem to die alone, but he establishes a community of believing followers at the foot of the cross.

After calling the community into existence, Jesus knows that all is completed. In the fourth scene, he brings the scriptures to fulfillment: He utters the very human cry, "I thirst" (19:28). It expresses his desire to fulfill his Father's will by drinking the cup of suffering and by his death completing the work of salvation. When he takes the wine, he declares, "It is finished," and then he hands over his spirit and dies. This Jesus, who calmly lays down his life, differs greatly from Mark's Jesus, who cries out in anguish, "My God, my God, why have you forsaken me?" (Mk 15:34). In freely handing over his spirit, Jesus breathes forth the Paraclete onto the small community gathered at the cross. His action recalls his words "If I do not go away, the Paraclete will never come to you" (16:7). It also foreshadows his giving the Holy Spirit to his disciples on Easter Sunday evening (20:22).

In Mark's gospel, Jesus' death is accompanied with dramatic signs: The Temple curtain is torn, and the Roman centurion professes faith in Jesus as the Son of God (Mk 15:38-39). In the fifth scene, John places before us a sign to be contemplated—the pierced body of Jesus (19:31-37). When his side is pierced, blood and water come forth; this recalls Jesus' earlier words, "From within shall flow rivers of living water" (7:38). This water symbolizes the Spirit to be given in Jesus' hour of glory. The blood and water signify that now that the hour has come, Jesus has passed from this world to the Father. He has been glorified, and so the Spirit is poured out on the community, represented by his mother and the beloved disciple. Clearly, the drama of the cross does not end in death but in a flow of life from death. Life for the community begins with Jesus' death. The early Church also understand the water and blood as symbols of baptism (water) and Eucharist (blood), through which life comes to the community.

In the sixth and final scene, attention is focused on the removal of Jesus' body from the cross, its preparation for burial, and its burial in a garden tomb (19:38-42). Nicodemus' appearance with Joseph of Arimathea recalls how he first came to Jesus by night to learn more about him (3:1-21) and how he spoke a favorable word on Jesus' behalf among his fellow Pharisees (7:51). Now Nicodemus comes forward in the daylight to identify with the community of disciples by performing the traditional burial duties for Jesus. Jesus' words are verified: "And I, when I am lifted up from the earth, will draw all men to myself" (12:32).

In Mark, Jesus' body is buried without being anointed with aromatic oils (Mk 16:1), but in John, Jesus is buried like a king, with a staggering amount of myrrh and aloes, and with his body bound in a cloth soaked in aromatic oils (19:39-40). Thus, throughout his passion and death Jesus is portrayed as a sovereign king who has overcome the world and who reigns in glory from the cross.

Several familiar themes run through the Johannine account of *the visit to the empty tomb and the Easter appearances of the risen Jesus* (20:1-31). In the earlier sections of the gospel, we watched Jesus as he revealed himself to his disciples, and we attended to the disciples' response, especially to what they saw and to how they moved from seeing to believing. Now, in Jesus' post-resurrection appearances to the disciples, he fulfills the promises made to them at the last supper—that he would return to them and bring them peace and joy, that he would send them into the world to witness by their love for one another, and that he would remain with them through the Paraclete.

When Mary Magdalene visits the tomb early Easter morning, she discovers the stone taken away and runs to tell Peter and the beloved disciple that Jesus' body had been stolen. The beloved disciple runs to the tomb ahead of Peter and stoops to see the linen clothes lying where Jesus' body had lain. Peter arrives and enters the tomb to see the same burial wrappings. The beloved disciple then follows Peter into the tomb, sees the wrappings again, knows that the body has not been stolen, and believes that Jesus is risen from the dead. Both men see the evidence, but only the beloved disciple moves from seeing to believing. In the wrappings he detects signs of his master's presence, even though he does not see Jesus himself. The beloved disciple, who sees through eyes of faith and love, represents the community created at the foot of the cross and stands in striking contrast to Thomas, who demands special signs before coming to faith (20:25).

After Peter and the beloved disciple depart, Mary sees two angels sitting in the tomb where Jesus' body has lain. She turns around and sees Jesus, but she mistakes him for the gardener until he reveals himself by calling her by name. She responds, *"Rabboni!"* (which means "teacher"). Since the risen Jesus had been transformed, Mary Magdalene does not recognize him until he chooses to reveal himself. Jesus is the same, but different. Mary Magdalene has felt depressed because he has been taken away, and she laments his absence. But she continues to look for him, and through a special revelation comes to recognize him as her risen Lord. She is a positive model of resurrection faith.

In holding Jesus, Mary expresses her desire for intimate union. But Jesus stops her. "Do not hold me, for I have not yet ascended to the Father" (20:17). Jesus assures Mary Magdalene that she will enjoy an intimate union with him, but only after he has completed his return to the Father to send the Holy Spirit. Through that Paraclete, "his own" will enter into union with their Lord. Jesus, transformed by his hour of glory, will share himself by dwelling within those who believe in him. Assured of this union, Mary Magdalene returns in haste to announce to the disciples, "I have seen the Lord" (20:18). Mary Magdalene contrasts with the women in Mark, who depart in fear from the empty tomb and say nothing to the disciples (Mark 16:8).

Next, Jesus comes to the frightened community of disciples through locked doors. He greets them, "Peace be with you" (20:19,21). Seen in the light of his promise to cast out fear and give them his peace, Jesus' words are filled with meaning. "Peace I leave with you; my peace I give to you; not as the world gives do I give to you. Let not your hearts be troubled, neither let them be afraid. You heard me say to you, 'I go away, and I will come to you'" (14:27-28). Jesus fulfills his promise by granting them a peace based on his abiding presence. The disciples hear his words, see his hands and his side, and respond with gladness. In doing so, they fulfill Jesus' promise that their sorrow at his leaving would turn into joy upon his return (16:20).

Jesus then entrusts the disciples with the mission given him by the Father. "As the Father has sent me, even so I send you" (20:21). Jesus was sent into the world as light to confront and challenge the darkness, and his disciples are to continue that mission through the quality of their self-sacrificing love (13:34-35). Jesus' love-command has formed them into a community identified to the world as his followers. Outsiders will recognize in the community a love distinguished by self-sacrifice, a love that challenges and confronts all those in darkness. And so Jesus sends the disciples to continue his mission, and he remains present with them precisely because it is his mission. Their mission, like his own, offers life and salvation to those who believe (6:39-40,57).

At the last supper Jesus promised that only after he had gone away would his disciples be able to receive the Paraclete (16:7). Now at his return, Jesus breathes on them, saying; "Receive the Holy Spirit" (20:22), and thereby he fulfills his repeated promises to send the Paraclete. He sends his disciples to continue his mission, and he gives them the Paraclete who will bear witness with them (15:26-27). In this context, the power to forgive sins or retain forgiveness resembles the Paraclete's role in convincing the world of sin, that is, of its refusal to believe in the revelation of the Father available in and through his son Jesus Christ (16:8-9).

In the final episode Thomas does not accept the disciples' word, "We have seen the Lord" (20:25). Instead, he demands to see in Jesus' hand the print of the nails, to place his finger in the mark of the nails and his hand in his side. Later, Jesus appears to Thomas. He meets Thomas' demands by telling him to see the print of the nails, to place his finger in the mark of the nails and his hand in Jesus' side. Thomas responds with a strong profession of faith: "My Lord and my God!" (20:28). Jesus commends Thomas, but he praises still more those in subsequent generations who accept Jesus as their Lord and God without seeing him or hearing his words—people like John and his community.

In this chapter we have explored the story of John's gospel, a story into which we are invited to enter through prayer and study. At the center Jesus moves as light into darkness to reveal himself as the Messiah and Son of Man, and as the universal and transcendent Son of God. As men and women encounter Jesus throughout the gospel story, they model different styles of response, from the hostility of the Jews to the faith of Thomas. We have watched Jesus wash his disciples' feet, and we have listened to him instruct his disciples about becoming children of God. He commands them to love one another as he has loved them, he promises them the Paraclete as his abiding presence, and he warns them to expect a permanent hostility from the world of darkness. Finally, we have entered to Jesus' hour of glory—his passion, death, resurrection, ascension, and the sending of the Paraclete. John invites us into this story to let it inform and influence our view of the world. He makes his intention clear with these concluding words:

Now Jesus did many other signs in the presence of the disciples, which are not written in this book; but these are written that you may believe that Jesus is the Christ, the Son of God, and that believing you may have life in his name (20:30-31).

Epilogue

In the gospels of Mark and John we read the same basic story about Jesus' ministry: about the network of relationships with his followers, the crowds, and the Jewish religious authorities, and about his death and resurrection. In telling the story, however, each evangelist creates a distinctive interpretation of its meaning. Each evangelist responds to the concrete experience of his community. Each offers images, symbols, metaphors, and stories that will help his community find in Jesus Christ— in his words and actions, in his death and resurrection—the true meaning of life. I want now to reflect on some of the more significant differences between Mark and John.

Mark's gospel was written immediately after the Jewish war (which ended A.D. 70) for Christian communities facing critical questions about their identity. The impact of the Jewish war, especially the destruction of Jerusalem and of the Temple, made the early Christians wonder about their place within Judaism. Mark addressed their confusion by showing that following Jesus means being ready to suffer as he suffered; it meant being dedicated to the mission Jesus gave them and waiting patiently in hope for his future coming as the triumphant Son of Man.

In contrast, John's gospel was written toward the end of the first century (A.D. 90-100) for diaspora communities, the majority of whom were Christian Jews. John's gospel addressed the tension that reached the breaking point over the Christian Jews' participation in the diaspora synagogues. Christian Jews were forced to choose between their Jewish heritage and their faith in Jesus as Messiah and Son of God. To encourage them, John presents Jesus as the one who replaced and completed the Jewish religious heritage. He portrays Jesus as engaged in a struggle with his fellow Jews, a struggle that strongly resembles the experience of John's community.

At times the historical setting of Mark, with its search for identity in a time of deep transition, may resemble our situation. At other times we may identify with the tension that John's community experienced with diaspora Jews. Or we may find elements of each situation in our experience. As we let these resemblances emerge, we begin to make meaningful contact with the communities for whom the gospels were written, a contact based on common human experience, a contact that can transcend the distance in time and the differences in culture.

In Mark, Jesus appears more human than divine as he announces and serves the Kingdom of God. By healing every disease and infirmity, Jesus demonstrates that the power of the Kingdom conquers all evil. Through teaching in parables, he teases the crowds into accepting the simple stories that reveal the mysteries of the Kingdom. And in a series of debates he confronts the Jewish religious authorities and easily reduces them to silence. Above all, Mark's Jesus is the Son of Man who exercises God's power in his ministry, who passes through suffering and death, who now sits at the right hand of power, and who will come in triumph to establish the Kingdom of God forever. Throughout Mark's gospel, Jesus demonstrates the apocalyptic struggle between God's kingly power at work in him and the evil powers at work in the world.

In contrast, John's gospel presents Jesus as one who existed prior to his appearance on earth, who became fully human in his life, ministry, and death, and who, when his work on earth was finished, returned to his home with God. John's Jesus is both human and divine, both at home and a stranger on earth. He talks, not about the Kingdom of God, but about himself as the Son of Man coming from God and going to God, as the revelation of the Father, as the Messiah and Son of God. Again and again through signs and words, John's Jesus reveals to his own people that he is sent by the Father. As light, he brings salvation into a world of darkness; he makes salvation available to those who choose to believe in him. Jesus' "signs" do not so much demonstrate God's power at work against the powers of evil as they symbolize and reveal that Jesus is sent by the Father. Jesus moves through his life, passion, and death in full command of every situation; he seems a stranger to human weakness and desolation.

In both Mark and John, Jesus is betrayed by Judas and arrested in the garden, abandoned by his followers and denied by

Peter, handed over to crucifixion by Pilate, mocked and scourged by Roman soldiers, and crucified with robbers. But the two death scenes reveal how differently these two gospels interpret the same event. In Mark, Jesus cries, "My God, my God, why hast thou forsaken me?" (15:34). Engulfed by darkness and overcome by evil powers, Jesus expresses the absence of God with a cry of utter weakness. He dies with this cry of desolation and without relief from the pressures against him. He has been deserted by his followers, taunted by his enemies, derided by his fellow criminals, and covered by darkness. He even feels abandoned by his Father. As king of the Jews, he dies a criminal's death. As the powerful Son of Man, he comes into that power through total weakness on the cross.

In a most striking contrast, John's Jesus reigns triumphantly from the cross. He knows that he has accomplished all that was given him by his Father. Bringing the scriptures to fulfillment, he utters the very human cry "I thirst" (19:28). He thirsts to fulfill his Father's will and by his death completes the work of salvation. When Jesus has taken the wine, he declares, "It is finished." Then, with no apparent pain or struggle, he calmly hands over his spirit and dies. In freely dying, Jesus breathes forth the Paraclete on the community of believers gathered at the cross and thereby anticipates the gift he will give his disciples on Easter evening. On the surface, Jesus' death is a crushing defeat and a disgraceful humiliation, but in reality it is his triumphant hour of glory.

What are we to make of such different portraits of Jesus? We might try to harmonize the two stories and blend them into one account. Such a harmony would, however, deny each gospel its uniqueness and destroy its distinctive portrait of Jesus. Once we recognize that Mark's Jesus differs from John's, we can begin to appreciate what each portrait tells us about Jesus. These two stories about Jesus' life, death, and resurrection complement and mutually enrich each other. If we allow each gospel to be itself and draw us into its story, we can learn through prayer and study to appreciate the symbols and metaphors that create that story, and we can begin to let each story carry meaning for our lives.

In Mark, the closest followers of Jesus—Peter, the Twelve, the women—are portrayed as faithful but also faithless, as understanding but also misunderstanding, as enthusiastic but also afraid. They fail to understand that following Jesus means participating in his work and sharing his power to preach and heal; it means accepting and living the mysterious paradox revealed in Jesus' passage through suffering and death to the glory of his resurrection and his final return in triumph. On the way to Jerusalem, Jesus predicts and enters into that paradox, and he instructs his disciples to expect their lives to be patterned according to the same paradox. The journey to Jerusalem begins the time of suffering and tribulation, but his followers are instructed to wait in hope for a glorious future to unfold. Salvation is more future than present, more "not yet" than "already here."

In contrast, John's Jesus continually confronts and challenges his people to recognize and believe in him as the one sent by the Father, as the one in and through whom they can see and know the Father. Faith in Jesus as a wonder-worker does not suffice for salvation; faith must move through amazement at Jesus' words and actions to acknowledging him as Son of God. As we have seen, John's gospel dramatizes a wide spectrum of responses, from the faith of the disciples to the disbelief of the Jewish religious authorities.

At the last supper, those who believe are told by Jesus that they are already God's children; they are expected to reproduce his self-sacrificing love by loving one another. Jesus then promises to send another Paraclete, and he instructs his own to follow the Paraclete's guidance and teaching. Jesus warns the disciples that they will be sent into the darkness to experience the same hostility Jesus experienced. But they should not fear, since as God's children they are already saved. In direct contrast to Mark's gospel, John presents salvation as more present than future, as more "already here" than "not yet here."

At one time we may find ourselves drawn more to Mark's story of Jesus and his followers, at other times to John's portrait of the dynamics of faith. As we move through life, we may also be attracted to different aspects of the same gospel. In childhood, for example, we begin to experience a new sense of belonging, and we more consciously join our immediate family. We love stories, with their concrete images and action, and we take them as literal expressions of real life. We may be drawn to the stories in Mark and John as central to our family's Christian heritage. We may need and want Jesus the Superman to move through our world as he moves through the quick, concise episodes in Mark. We want this Jesus of heroic power over evil to make the bad people good, the sick people well, and the dead people alive. We may find John's story more difficult, since we easily lose the action in the discourses and dialogues. Within the story, however, we may find meaning in Jesus' actions for others—changing water into wine, cleansing the Temple, healing the royal official's son, healing the man at the pool of Siloam, multiplying bread, walking on the water, healing the man born blind, raising Lazarus from the dead. We marvel at how Jesus shows compassion for others and expresses heroic power to rescue them from embarrassment, illness, or death. The dramatic qualities in John's passion narrative may also appeal to children, since Jesus is a triumphant hero even in apparent defeat.

As young adults, we may tend to interpret our lives along conventional lines. We are anxious to respond faithfully to the expectations and judgments of significant others, such as our spouse, respected persons at work, or church officials. Authority resides in such trustworthy persons, and we place high value on these significant relationships. Our prayer life at this stage of maturity will naturally reflect these same concerns. We might experience ourselves attracted to the person of Jesus Christ, and we might desire that he become a significant person in our lives. When we read Mark and John we may feel drawn to passages in which Jesus invites persons into relationships with himself. We may focus on Mark's portrayal of Jesus calling the disciples, choosing twelve to be with him and share in his work, instructing them on the meaning of the parables, and drawing them into a more intimate friendship with himself. Then again, we might find special meaning in John's stories about Jesus as a significant other for John the Baptist, the disciples, the Samaritan woman, the man born blind, Mary and Martha, Thomas. In a word, we may see Jesus as a personal authority and may be attracted to portrayals of him that invite and challenge us to share his life and values and to participate in his work.

As we begin to rely less on conventional authorities and take personal responsibility for our commitments, life-style, beliefs, and attitudes, we may find ourselves drawn to the either/or polarities in these gospels, to the apocalyptic struggle between good and evil in Mark and to the continual confrontation between light and darkness in John. In Mark the miracle stories can show us how God's power in Jesus triumphs over the evil powers in the sick and possessed, and the debate stories set Jesus in sharp conflict with the accepted religious conventions. John's gospel, with its radical dualism, discloses to us a sharply dichotomized world. As we grow in the ability to stand alone as individuals and with a small group of like-minded people to choose our own way of making meaning in our lives, we may find ourselves drawn to the elements in Mark and John that call for decision.

As we reach our middle years, we may embrace and affirm the paradoxes and polarities of life and learn to live with complexity and ambiguity. We may begin to know from experience the meaning of defeat and disappointment and to experience the reality of irrevocable commitments. Because life itself has taught us the paradoxes of life in death, hope in despair, joy in suffering, power in weakness, we are able to read Mark and John attentive to this central paradox. In Mark we see Jesus passing through suffering and death to glory. In John we grow to appreciate the irony in dramatic scenes such as the cure of the blind man, the raising of Lazarus, and the trial before Pilate. These scenes demonstrate that what happens on the surface of the story is not the true reality and that the true reality is available only to those who penetrate to the deeper mysterious, sometimes paradoxical meaning.

Mark and John can, then, accompany us through life. In this book I have introduced you to these two gospels, invited you to pray with them, and showed you how to study their worlds. When we pray, we desire to encounter the risen Lord. When we study, we want to learn more about these gospels. I am convinced that praying with Mark and John will awaken in you the desire to study, that studying Mark and John will enrich your prayer, and that through both prayer and study you will deepen your religious appreciation of these writings. If this book has drawn you to pray with Mark and John and has awakened in you the desire to learn more about them, it has accomplished the purpose for which it was written.